The Early Alphabet

D1533162

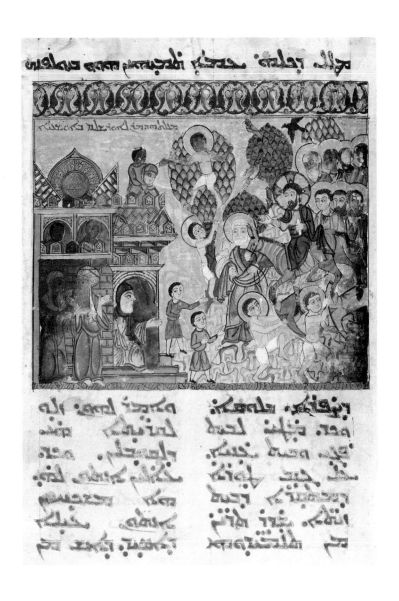

Esṭrangelā Syriac illuminated Gospel Lectionary (Christ's Entry into Jerusalem), AD 1216–20. BL Add 7170 f115a

The Early Alphabet

John F. Healey

University of California Press/British Museum

Note on Transcription

As a general convention within the text, individual *sounds* as part of the language concerned are represented by letters placed between two slashes (e.g. /th/), while *letters* – when the reference is, for example, to their shape in written form or to their position in the alphabet – appear either as capitals (upper case) or as small (lower case) forms *without* slashes (e.g. Latin G/g; Greek Γ/γ). Capitals are often preferred, since the lower case forms arose at a late date and lack significant ancient features which it is often helpful to represent visually.

Acknowledgements

In a survey covering such a wide field the author has been conscious of the need to take advice from various specialists and would in particular like to thank Mr A. R. Millard (University of Liverpool) for many helpful comments and Professor G. R. Smith (University of Manchester) for advice on Arabic and South Arabian. Errors which remain are, of course, entirely the responsibility of the author. Illustrations are reproduced by courtesy of the Trustees of the Chester Beatty Library, Dublin (fig. 21); the Musée du Louvre, Paris (figs. 17, 22, 23, 35); the British Library (figs. 24, 28, 31, 33, 39, 40, frontispiece), and the British Museum (figs. 1, 4, 5, 10, 13, 14, 18, 19, 26, 30); and from the following works by permission of the publishers: D. Pardee, *Les textes para-mythologiques de la 24e campagne*, Éditions Recherche sur les Civilisations, Paris, 1988 (fig. 6); C. Virolleaud, *Le palais royal d'Ugarit* II, Imprimerie Nationale/Librairie C. Klincksieck, Paris, 1957 (fig. 8); *Revue Biblique* 93 (1986) (fig. 9); A. F. L. Beeston, *Sabaic Grammar*, University of Manchester, 1984 (fig. 11); H. Donner and W. Röllig, *Kanaanäische und Aramäische Inschriften* III, Otto Harrassowitz, Wiesbaden, 1969 (fig. 12); K. Jaroš, *Hundert Inschriften aus Kanaan und Israel*, Schweizerisches Katholisches Bibelwerk, Fribourg, 1982 (fig. 20); I. J. Gelb, *A Study of Writing*, University of Chicago Press, 1963 (fig. 25); D. Diringer, *The Alphabet*, Hutchinson, London, 1968 (fig. 27); T. O. Lambdin, *Introduction to Classical Ethiopic (Ge'ez)*, Scholars Press, Missoula, 1978 (fig. 32); *Manuscripts of the Middle East*, Ter Lugt Press, Leiden, 1990 (figs. 36, 37); Y. H. Safadi, *Islamic Calligraphy*, Thames and Hudson, London, 1978 (fig. 38).

University of California Press
Berkeley and Los Angeles

© 1990 The Trustees of the British Museum

Designed by John Hawkins

Printed in Great Britain

Volume 9 in the *Reading the Past* series

Library of Congress Cataloging-in-Publication Data

Healey, John F.
  The early alphabet/John F. Healey. — 1st U.S. ed.
     p.   cm. — (Reading the past : 9)
  Includes bibliographical references and index.
  ISBN 0–520–07309–6 (paper)
  1. Alphabet—History. 2. Writing—History.
  I. Title. II. Series.
P211.H44 1991   90–40443
411—dc20   CIP

Contents

Preface

This book attempts to summarise the general scholarly consensus of views on the early history of alphabetic writing. Inevitably it is necessary to abbreviate and simplify the arguments. Even major issues are often still the subject of dispute. A whole book of over 350 pages has recently been devoted solely to the discussion of early cuneiform alphabets, while in the present volume only a few pages could be given over to this topic!

The origin of alphabetic writing is one of those historical questions which is of interest to all peoples of European, Middle Eastern and Indian origin or educated in the Christian, Jewish or Islamic traditions. For all of us, the alphabet is the first thing we learnt from our parents or our teachers. It is the foundation on which all our subsequent education was based. For many it is also the vehicle of divine revelation, though in fact, as we shall see, the alphabet is one of the many gifts which the great 'book' religions and their associated civilisations owe to the *pagan* world.

The account of the alphabet which follows begins with the discussion of the basic principles involved in alphabetic writing. This is accompanied by a brief description of the characteristics of the Semitic languages for which the alphabet was first used: apart from enabling the reader to understand the problems involved in the devising of the alphabet, this provides a useful reminder that not all languages are alike and that the problems of writing them may vary considerably.

Next, evidence for the earliest attempts at alphabetic writing is outlined. Only one of these attempts was really successful and the third chapter deals with this in detail and with the transmission of this alphabet to the Greeks and ultimately to the Latin West.

The rest of the book is concerned mostly with the ways the alphabet developed later in the Semitic world, leaving behind certain backwaters which continued to exist while the mainstream moved on. The mainstream produced the Jewish (often called the Hebrew) script and the Arabic script. The latter, along with the Latin script, may be regarded as the culmination of a major historical phase in which writing by means of a relatively simple alphabetic system became the foundation of European and Middle Eastern culture, replacing the oral traditions which had existed for millennia before.

Whereas paper and ink may shortly become obsolete, it seems likely that the alphabet, on screen rather than on paper, will remain important for a long time yet. On the other hand, it seems unlikely that our electronic 'writings' are going to survive as long as the earliest alphabetic inscriptions, which were written around 1700 BC and are still today the subject of much lively scholarly interest.

1
Script, Language and the Alphabetic Principle

There is a big difference between script and language, though they tend to be confused. A language consists of a system of sounds. It does not have to be written down. Indeed languages were spoken for millennia before writing was invented and there are still today some unwritten languages (e.g. in India and South America). Any particular language can be represented more or less satisfactorily in any system of writing. One could invent a new system of writing one's own language but one would have to face up to the difficulty of reconciling several conflicting demands on the system. One such demand is the need to keep things simple, so that the new writing system is not so complex as to be unlearnable, but there is also a need to represent all the sounds of the language distinctively, so that the system is unambiguous.

The writing systems of the ancient Near East prior to the invention and spread of the alphabet from *c.* 1700 BC onwards included a large number of syllabic signs, i.e. with each sign representing a syllable. They were developed from forms of pictographic writing in which small pictures stood for objects and concepts. These had been in use, principally in Egypt and Mesopotamia, since before 3000 BC. Syllabic writing became widespread and new forms of syllabic writing continued to be developed (e.g. Hittite, Cretan, Byblian).

A syllable normally consists of at least two sounds, most commonly a consonant followed by a vowel. Since all languages have far more possible syllables than they have individual sounds (/ba/, /be/, /bi/, /bo/, /bu/, /da/, /de/, /di/, /do/, /du/ are all separate syllables), syllabic systems involved a very large number of signs. The total number of cuneiform signs in the system used in Mesopotamia, for example, is almost six hundred, though some of these retain a pictographic type of function, representing whole words. Many signs had more than one sound-value. Fortunately much smaller repertoires of signs and restricted variations of value were current at any one time and the context would usually show what was intended.

As we will see, the credit for the devising of the alphabetic principle in writing cannot be ascribed to any particular individual, though Greek tradition credited the introduction of the alphabet to Greece to the legendary Kadmos and the Phoenicians. Some scholars would prefer to avoid thinking in terms of an individual inventor, but unless we think of an individual discovering the alphabet, like a Newton or an Einstein, we are in danger of undervaluing the greatness of the achievement.

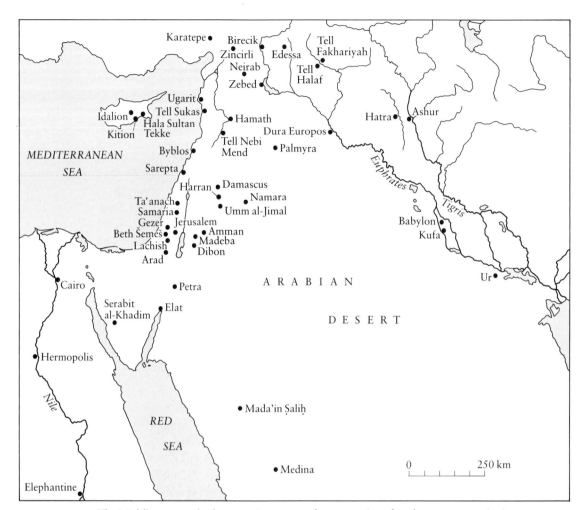

The Middle East (only the more important places mentioned in the text are marked).

This achievement is essentially the insight that writing would be most easily organised if each distinct single sound of a particular language were represented by a single distinctive sign. Since the number of separate sounds is in most languages rather small, the number of signs needed is also rather small – about forty at the most. If we compare this with the writing systems already then in existence (though it seems unlikely that the inventor of the alphabet was an expert in any of these older systems) it implies a glorious simplification. We may note also that the idea of isolating individual sounds has stood the test of time and is still basic to modern linguistics.

Apart from its cumbersomeness, the Akkadian system was unsatisfactory for another reason. It was devised originally not for Akkadian at all but for

Sumerian, and it is often called Sumero-Akkadian. Sumerian is a completely unrelated language lacking some of the distinctive sounds which are essential to Akkadian, so that some of these Akkadian sounds are not properly represented in the script. The inventor of the alphabet on the other hand was able to devise a sign to represent each of the sounds he needed in the (Semitic) language he was intending to write.

Having thus far praised our notional inventor, we must next remark that he did not do quite so thorough a job as he might have done, since he only isolated consonantal sounds and made no allowance at all for vowels. In fact all the ancient Near Eastern alphabets which followed from the first devising of the alphabet are not really alphabets in our modern sense. They are consonantal alphabets and the vowels were only fully represented in these alphabets at a very late date (AD). There were *some* earlier attempts to represent vowels, since in Aramaic and then in Hebrew script certain consonants, particularly **h, w** and **y**, came to be used in limited circumstances to represent vowels, i.e. as vowel-letters. Compare English words like 'very' in which y is used as a vowel, though it is normally treated as a consonant as in 'yes'.

In principle it is not unthinkable to write English without vowels. Native speakers of English would be able to add the correct vowels in pronunciation without too much difficulty most of the time. The reader could test this statement by reading it without vowels: Ntv spkrs f nglsh wld b bl t dd th crrct vwls n prnnctn wtht t mch dffclty mst f th tm. In English the main difficulty arises with words *beginning* with a vowel, a difficulty which was less serious in West Semitic scripts since no words began with vowels. Difficulties might well arise also with personal and geographical names, especially names unfamiliar to most readers, but otherwise much would depend on the ability of the reader to apprehend the context of what was being said. It should be remembered that modern newspapers in Hebrew and Arabic are still printed for the most part without vowels and the native speakers of these languages have no difficulty in reading them.

It may be noted that at least one prominent scholar, I. J. Gelb, took the view that this consonantal alphabet is not in fact a true alphabet but should be regarded as a syllabary in which each sign stands for a consonant followed by any vowel. This is a defensible view, but it involves a rather narrow definition of what constitutes an alphabet and it may result in the genius of the consonantal alphabet being undervalued.

However, the true alphabet in our modern sense came into existence when the Greeks, who seem to have got their idea of the alphabet *and* the main letter-forms from the Phoenicians, began to use certain signs, ones which they did not need for consonants in Greek, to represent the vowels. Subsequently the Near Eastern scripts underwent modifications to allow vowels to be expressed either by the addition of special vowel-letters (see above) or by the addition of marks above and below the consonants or, in the case of Ethiopic, by the devising of modifications to the consonants to indicate which particular vowel follows.

There is another aspect of the study of the alphabet which needs brief introduction: the development and fixing of the order of the letters. Surprisingly, perhaps, there is a considerable amount of evidence on this matter even from the earliest times. There are even texts which simply list the letters in the alphabetic order. On the analogy of our ordering of the alphabet as the ABC (pronounced 'ay-bee-cee-dee', etc.), such texts are called 'abecedaries', though the actual ordering may not be the same as ours. (The letter C, as we shall see, was peculiar to Latin and has no real equivalent in the old alphabets.) Information on the alphabetic order is not of purely antiquarian interest: in a number of cases it gives useful information on how the alphabet itself developed. We shall see that the very ordering of both the Ugaritic and the Greek alphabets reveals that certain letters were added secondarily.

Finally, we may note the intrinsic importance of the names of the letters in the different languages. Reflection on the English names of the letters will reveal that this is quite a complicated matter. Why do speakers of British English call **Z** 'zed', while Americans, apparently with greater logic, call it 'zee', like 'bee' and 'dee'? And why 'el' for **L** and 'aitch' for **H**? In the ancient languages the names of the letters can be very important for reconstructing the particular source from which the alphabet was borrowed. For example, the name of the first letter of the Greek alphabet, *alpha* (ἄλφα), is Semitic, like the names of virtually all the letters of the Greek alphabet.

The Semitic Languages

The term 'Semitic' is an accident in the history of scholarship in this field, which arose from an assumed connection with Shem, the son of Noah. It was coined in the eighteenth century AD to refer to a group of languages of which Hebrew and Arabic were the best-known constituents. Today one might prefer a different term, perhaps geographical ('Western Asiatic' or 'Syro-Arabian'), but all other terms have drawbacks and 'Semitic' is convenient and traditional.

Semitic languages were not so widely dispersed as the members of the Indo-European family, but our knowledge of Semitic has great depth in the sense that we possess detailed knowledge of many ancient as well as modern Semitic languages reaching back to the third millennium BC.

The first Semitic language on record is Akkadian which was used in Mesopotamia (basically modern Iraq) under the great empires of the Babylonians and Assyrians. The writing was cuneiform (i.e. with signs formed from patterns of wedges in soft clay) and syllabic. The use of this language in its various dialects continued down to the time of Christ. It had, however, come under strong pressure from Aramaic, another Semitic language, which had its origins in the late second millennium BC and was the language of the Aramaeans.

West Semitic	East Semitic
Eblaite (classification unresolved)	Akkadian:
Ugaritic	*Old Akkadian*
Canaanite: *Phoenician and Punic*	*Babylonian*
Hebrew	*Assyrian*
Moabite, Edomite, etc.	
Aramaic: *Early Aramaic*	
Persian Empire Aramaic	
Nabataean	
Hatran	
Palmyrene	
Jewish Aramaic	
Samaritan Aramaic	
Syriac	
Mandaic	
Modern Aramaic dialects	

South Semitic

Pre-Islamic South Arabian:
  Sabaic, etc.
Pre-Islamic northern dialects:
  Thamudic, Lihyanite, Safaitic, etc.
Arabic
Modern South Arabian:
  Mehrī, etc.
Ethiopian: *Classical Ethiopic (Ge'ez)*
  Amharic, etc.

Table summarising the main divisions of the Semitic language group.

The Aramaean people lived mostly in Syria and upper Mesopotamia and they were using an alphabetic script for their writings. The Aramaic language and script spread rapidly throughout the region. It was used by the great imperial powers of the time and, in the period of the Persian Empire (*c.* 550–323 BC), Aramaic and its script were used by the imperial administration and throughout the western provinces of the Empire as far as Arabia and Egypt.

    Aramaic gradually replaced other local languages in Syria/Palestine, languages such as Phoenician (which had an important predecessor in the local language of ancient Ugarit on the Syrian coast *c.* 1500–1200 BC) and Hebrew, which was little used after Old Testament times, though there is some dispute about whether Hebrew became extinct as a spoken language before or after the time of Christ. A number of local dialects of Aramaic became established in important centres. Thus Aramaic became the normal language both of the Jewish communities in the Middle East and of the various 'pagan' kingdoms, like that of the Nabataeans centred on Petra in Jordan. As the pagans were converted and the Christian church spread to the east, Aramaic became its official language, more specifically the dialect of Aramaic known as Syriac (originally the Aramaic dialect of Edessa, modern Urfa/Şanlıurfa in southern Turkey).

After Akkadian and Aramaic, the next great linguistic upheaval in the region came with the dramatic spread of Arabic at the time of the Islamic conquests in the seventh century AD. Arabic remains the main language of the Middle East and the main modern representative of Semitic, though there are also some other living Semitic languages: Amharic (the main Semitic language of Ethiopia), various southern Arabian dialects, remnants of Aramaic (still spoken in parts of Syria, Turkey, Iraq and the USSR) and, of course, modern Israeli Hebrew, which has returned to the Middle East as a spoken language relatively recently.

Since they are relevant to some extent to questions of script, it will be useful to note some major characteristics of the Semitic languages. The first is that all the Semitic languages contain sounds which do not exist in English and other European languages. An example is the so-called emphatic /t/, which is difficult for English-speakers to master. To produce it involves pronouncing the English /t/ but with the tongue flaccid instead of rigid and slightly pressed up towards the roof of the mouth. It is a thickened /t/ of the kind we associate with intoxication or a dental anaesthetic. Since this sound does not exist in English or in our script (which is really the Latin script with a few modifications), linguists have to represent this consonant with a conventional sign to make it clear that it is not the ordinary /t/ which is in question. The convention widely accepted is to place a dot under the ordinary /t/, i.e. /ṭ/. There are other special sounds which need not be explained here, but the variety of signs likely to be encountered in studying the alphabets used for the Semitic languages include such extras as / ḍ/, / ṣ/, / ṭ/, /ġ/, /ʾ/, /ʿ/ and /š/. The Semitic scripts also often distinguish long from short vowels and this distinction is usually represented by the placing of a line over the vowel in our Latin script to mark the long variety: /ā/, /ī/, /ū/. When we give the equivalent in our own script for the letters in a word of one of the other scripts (for example, Hebrew שָׁלוֹם = šālōm), the process is called transliteration.

The other relevant point is that consonants in verbal roots have a special role in all Semitic languages. They are not more important than vowels, as is often quite erroneously stated, but in many words the vowels carry out the grammatical job of giving precise meaning to a form, while the consonants are the 'root' and have attached to them the basic notion which is common to all the words based on that particular set of consonants. Thus there is an Arabic root *KTB*. *KTB* does not mean anything as it stands. Indeed it is totally unpronounceable. But by adding vowels in different patterns (and sometimes special prefixes), the root *KTB* comes to life and takes on meaning as a real word in the language: *kātib* means 'writer', *kataba* 'he wrote', *kitāb* 'book', *kutub* 'books', *kutubī* 'bookseller', *kitāba* 'writing', *maktab* 'office', and *maktaba* 'library, bookshop'. Observing these words we can confirm that there is a root *KTB* and deduce that it has to do with 'writing'. Thus the consonants are the bones which convey the basic meaning, while the vowels add flesh to the skeleton.

From this it is clear why some scholars connect the consonantal alphabet with the distinctive role played by consonants in Semitic word-formation. One should not, however, conclude that the ancient Semitic peoples used a conson-antal alphabet because vowels were unimportant to them. They were *very* important. Indeed, the best-attested ancient Semitic language, Akkadian, is written in a syllabic script taken over from Sumerian which *does* indicate vow-els, while the other important literary languages – Hebrew, Syriac, Arabic and Ethiopic – all eventually developed ways of expressing vowels in writing.

What one could, perhaps, say of the early consonantal alphabet is that it handled the root aspect of word-formation well, but was defective in that it failed to account satisfactorily for vowels, the other important ingredient in word-formation. The separation of consonants and vowels in the alphabet could, therefore, be said to correspond to the separation of function of vowels and consonants in the Semitic languages.

Writing Materials and Types of Script

The basic data for our study of the early alphabet are very varied. There are large public monumental inscriptions, burial inscriptions, private letters, coins, seals, casual graffiti, legal documents, literary works and, of course, Bibles and Qur'āns. The material on which the writing was executed also varied considerably and it could have an important influence on the development of the script. Much depended on local availability of materials. In Egypt papyrus was the typical material for most purposes. In Mesopotamia soft clay was used and subsequently dried or baked. Public monuments in both areas were usually of stone.

It is clear that the cuneiform writing system, using signs formed by patterns of wedge-shaped marks (Latin *cuneus* 'wedge'), was particularly suited to impression on soft clay. This style of writing could be imitated in stone but would be very difficult to use on papyrus. It is angular and sharp because of the type of stylus which was used, a cut reed. Cuneiform did spread westwards to Anatolia, Syria and Egypt and was used, as we shall see, for writing one of the earliest alphabets, but the major developments in alphabetic writing occurred not on clay tablets, but on the smooth dry surface of papyrus, dressed stone and pot.

Ancient papyrus is rarely preserved since, unlike dried clay tablets, which are very durable when buried in the earth, in most climatic conditions papyrus tends to rot and so disappear. Thus, although it is likely that papyrus was used extensively for writing in Phoenicia, Syria and Palestine, little has survived from those areas. Egypt, however, is one of the places where the climate sometimes allows preservation of papyrus (away from the river Nile itself) and we are fortunate in having some important collections of documents from there. Writing material produced from animal skins also is rarely preserved, though it *was* used, as were wax writing-boards. Inscriptions on stone are more durable, though vulnerable to shattering, grinding and weathering, and the same is true of writing on pieces of broken pot, commonly used in Palestine and elsewhere. An inscribed potsherd is called an ostracon (plural ostraca). Papyrus and pot were probably used side by side in Palestine as they were in Egypt, where papyrus was used, for example, for Aramaic legal and literary documents. Pot tended to be used as a cheap substitute for papyrus in writing ephemeral documents such as lists, notes, etc.

Epigraphy is the term generally used for the study of inscriptions carved or scratched on hard materials. In the study of regions where there are a lot of papyri preserved, the term palaeography tends to be restricted to the study of papyri only, though the distinction between writing on papyrus and writing on hard materials is really artificial. Both are part and parcel of a community's 'epigraphic' remains. In relation to Semitic inscriptions, it is common to use the term palaeography for a particular aspect of the study of writing on all materials, i.e. the study of the progressive developments and changes in the forms of the letters or signs. In the early history of writing, a fundamental development is the step from pictographic to linear forms in which the original pictographic intention has been forgotten or is very secondary. Forms thus become stylised and take on a life of their own, unrelated to the need to represent a pictured object.

Another broad distinction which should be noted is that between formal and cursive forms of writing. Normally the primary form of a writing system is that used for accounts, letters and lists, even if these are carefully produced by civil servants. The making of great public inscriptions is a secondary affair and would hardly happen without the prior existence of a strong tradition of 'normal' writing. The standardised, formal and decorative forms used especially for public monuments are usually called 'monumental'. A monumental script often gains a life of its own, becoming a separate script.

By contrast, the term 'cursive' is used for the type of script which is typically written at great speed. It is rounded rather than square, flowing and joined up (ligatured). The most cursive forms of script generally appear in the most casual pieces of writing. At its extreme this might be a traveller scratching his name on a rock-face while sitting to rest. This is called a graffito (plural graffiti). But we have to be careful. If this traveller has visited places where he has seen formal inscriptions, he might introduce monumental features into his graffito in order to make it look more impressive. Often monumental features are archaising features, which might deceive us in our attempt to date the text on palaeographic grounds. We see informal scripts particularly in letters and practical documents, though again there may be a degree of formality even within the cursive tradition.

It is also often possible to see the influence of the cursive style on the monumental style. Developments in the cursive style eventually cause changes in the monumental style. Thus even in the 'monumental' style of our own alphabet (e.g. on foundation stones and in print) the old-fashioned **g** with a closed loop hanging from the left of the upper circle is disappearing, just as it has mostly disappeared in handwriting. Nobody actually writes postcards to friends in the letter-style used in a printed book or on a foundation stone. Very few people, for example, reproduce the 'printed' form of lower-case **a** in their handwriting, or write without joining any of the letters.

The question of the direction of writing – right to left *v.* left to right, etc. – will be discussed where it arises, but it should at least be noted here that scripts can follow different conventions and may go through periods of uncertainty, using several methods side by side. Also, our convention of separating words with spaces is not found in all the traditions discussed here. Some separate words with special markers. Greek tended not to separate words at all. Most of the scripts we shall deal with habitually join certain words together. The word 'and' and also some prepositions are thus attached directly to the following word. And only at a rather late stage did the convention creep in of marking the ends of sentences.

2
First Attempts at Alphabetic Writing

There is evidence of attempts to write early West Semitic languages in a *local* syllabic script, i.e. neither in Mesopotamian cuneiform nor in Egyptian hieroglyphs. Such attempts have been identified in very early, second-millennium BC, inscriptions from Byblos in Lebanon and from Jordan. Unfortunately, the evidence is not very extensive and the interpretation of the material extremely uncertain.

The first steps towards *alphabetic* writing appear also to have been taken in the early second millennium BC. There is uncertainty about the order of events and precise dating, but a number of inscriptions have been discovered in Sinai and Palestine (and called Proto-Sinaitic or Proto-Canaanite) in which it appears that the Egyptian way of writing has been converted into an alphabetic system.

The Invention of the Consonantal Alphabet

The Egyptian system is essentially syllabic though, unlike Akkadian cuneiform, the vowel in any syllable is not defined. Thus there were, in Egyptian, signs representing **b** plus any vowel, **d** plus any vowel, etc. It appears that ultimately the signs used for these single-consonant signs derived from pictographs, though through the course of time the 'picture' came to represent not the object concerned but the first consonant of the Egyptian word for this object. Thus the sign for 'mouth', , originally pronounced as the word for 'mouth', *r* or *r'i*, came to be used for **r** plus any vowel or none. The principle of using a sign to represent the first letter of the word it stands for is called acrophony ('initial sound'). This gave the Egyptians the ready possibility of alphabetic writing, since in essence this kind of consonant-only system was all that was used for the alphabetic scripts which *did* develop. However, the Egyptians themselves did not take this step, and multi-consonant signs continued to be the basis of the Egyptian script.

The writers of the Proto-Sinaitic or Proto-Canaanite inscriptions apparently *did* take this step in the early to middle second millennium BC. The evidence is difficult and scholars do not agree on all points. The texts in question first became well known through a series of short inscriptions of *c.* 1700 BC onwards, carved by miners at the turquoise mines at Serabit al-Khadim in Sinai. Because the number of signs in these inscriptions was so small (less than thirty), it quickly became clear that this script was an alphabet and not a syllabary.

1

1 Sandstone sphinx with Proto-Sinaitic alphabetic inscription on its base. From Serabit al-Khadim, *c.* 1700 BC. BM WA 41748

Subsequently, other examples have been found in Palestine (Shechem, Gezer, Lachish), so we can be certain that we are dealing with a fairly widespread phenomenon. While we can never hope to know who invented the new so-called linear alphabet, two things seem clear. Firstly, there is clearly an Egyptian inspiration behind the invention, since there are some similarities of signs and the basic acrophonic principle (which has no parallel in cuneiform) must have come from knowledge of the Egyptian script. Secondly, the texts are in Canaanite West Semitic, not Egyptian, so we can be fairly sure of an origin of the script in the Semitic area which had close cultural contact with Egypt. Palestine is currently the strongest candidate, though the importance of the Phoenician coast (especially cosmopolitan Byblos) in the script traditions leads one to suspect that that region may have played a major role, just as it had produced a syllabic script of its own and eventually produced Ugaritic and Phoenician.

Basically the new script, which has been deciphered with a fair degree of certainty (though the texts are not always understood), uses the *Semitic* (not the Egyptian) word for the object of the original pictograph as the starting

2,3

2 Examples of Proto-Sinaitic: each group of letters reads (*l*)*b*'*lt*, 'for the goddess Ba'alat'.

3 Some Proto-Sinaitic forms.

⟆	'–'*alpu* ('ox')
⊐	b–*bētu* ('house')
⸮	w–*wawwu* ('hook/peg')
Ⅲ	ḥ–*ḫōtu* ('fence' ?)
⨆	k–*kappu* ('palm of hand')
⸑	l–*lamdu* ('goad')
∿	m–*mayyūma* (?) ('water')
⸏	n–*naḥašu* ('snake')
⊘	'–'*ēnu* ('eye')
⸐	r–*ra'šu* ('head')
✝	t–*tawwu* ('mark' ?)

point and uses the first letter of *that* word as the value of the sign. Thus the drawing of a house stood for 'house'. 'House' in West Semitic was *bēt*. Hence the 'house' pictograph was used for the consonant **b**. The acrophonic principle may not explain all the signs, but the following are clear: ' from *'alpu*, 'ox'; **b** from *baytu/bētu*, 'house'; **w** from *wawwu*, 'hook/peg'(?); **y** from *yadu* 'hand/arm'; **k** from *kappu*, 'palm of hand'; **l** from *lamdu*, 'goad'; **m** from *mayyūma* (?), 'water'; **n** from *naḥašu*, 'snake'; ' from *'aynu/'ēnu* 'eye'; and **r** from *ra'šu*, 'head' (original pronunciations partially conjectural).

While the Proto-Sinaitic/Proto-Canaanite inscriptions are quite obscure, there are some later Proto-Canaanite texts which are better understood (e.g. the thirteenth-century BC Lachish ewer, an ostracon of the twelfth century BC from Beth Šemeš, and the 'Izbet Ṣarṭah inscription, also of the twelfth century) and, although the material we have in this type of writing is very limited, it is clear from comparison of many of the letters with the much better known Phoenician script that the Phoenician is the direct descendant of the Proto-Sinaitic/Proto-Canaanite. Intermediate forms are found in a variety of small inscriptions from Palestine (the el-Khader arrowheads, twelfth century BC) and Lebanon (two in Proto-Canaanite and two in Phoenician). There are even fragments from as far away as Crete and Sardinia (eleventh century BC),

4 Phoenician inscribed arrowhead (front and back), 11th century BC. BM WA 136753

which should be especially noted in connection with the spread of the Semitic alphabet to the Greeks (discussed below).

As we shall see, the Hebrew, Aramaic and Greek scripts depend, at least according to the common view, on the Phoenician. From the Greek came our Latin alphabet and the Cyrillic (Russian) script, and from the Aramaic came the Arabic script and most of the scripts used in India. Thus from the Proto-Sinaitic/Proto-Canaanite alphabet came the writing systems of a large proportion of the modern world's population, Chinese being the main exception. Although we do not know who invented the new alphabet, the cultural advance it constituted is enormously significant.

The Ugaritic and Similar Alphabets

Other experiments in alphabet creation were going on at roughly the same time in northern Syria and Palestine; we know this from a number of finds, but principally from the archives of the ancient city of Ugarit, modern Ras Shamra (see map p. 8). From 1929 onwards, large numbers of inscribed clay tablets were found in excavations at the site. These are dated to the Late Bronze Age c. 1400–1200 BC and, while many were written in the familiar syllabic cuneiform of Akkadian and Hittite, some were written in a previously unknown 5,6

5 Ugaritic literary tablet.
BM loan 84 (AO 17.325) reverse

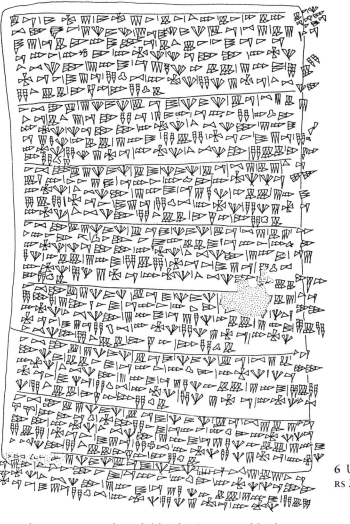

6 Ugaritic tablet:
RS 24.244r

cuneiform script (i.e. based, like the Sumero-Akkadian script, on wedge shapes) written from left to right. H. Bauer, E. Dhorme and C. Virolleaud worked on its decipherment at the same time, the first two having been engaged (on opposite sides!) in cipher work during World War I.

The decipherers worked in different ways, but what follows will give a basic idea of the kinds of logic used. It was quickly realised that the new script, despite being cuneiform, was alphabetic, since it clearly had only thirty signs in all. This was the basic working assumption. A second assumption, derived from knowledge of the linguistic history of the region, was that the language was probably West Semitic, akin to Phoenician and Hebrew, using like them a consonantal alphabet. These assumptions lead one to expect certain typical West Semitic prefixes and suffixes as well as, for example, traditional West Semitic ways of writing introductory formulae. Also it was noticed that a special sign was frequently used as a word-separator, just as we separate words by leaving a space between them.

Several texts and some brief inscriptions began with the same sign – 𐎍 . Thus we find 𐎍 𐎁 𐎓 𐎍 and 𐎍 𐎅 𐎋 𐎆 . Since there is a well-known West Semitic formula of using the preposition /l/, 'for, concerning', in the titles of texts and in ownership marks, it was guessed that 𐎍 stood for l. Similarly /-m/ and /-t/ are very common West Semitic endings used to mark plurals and feminine gender. Signs 𐎎 and 𐎚 seemed to fit the bill, since they occurred frequently at the ends of words. The group 𐎘 𐎍 𐎘 occurred a number of times. This is a very rare pattern in West Semitic (i.e. initial and final consonants of a word identical). The only likely candidate was the word for 'three', *šlš*, so it was supposed that 𐎘 represented /š/ (a supposition which was later refined to /t̠/, a sound not preserved in Phoenician and Hebrew, where it merged with /š/). Further guesswork led to the identification of 𐎍 𐎁 𐎓 𐎍 as *lb'l*, 'to (the god) Ba'al', and 𐎎 𐎍 𐎋 (𐎎) as *mlk(m)*, 'king(s)'. By this kind of procedure and with little delay, all the signs were identified and the language was confirmed to be a West Semitic one related to the later Phoenician and Hebrew languages.

7

'a	𐎀	k	𐎋
'i	𐎛	l	𐎍
'u	𐎜	m	𐎎
b	𐎁	n	𐎐
g	𐎂	s	𐎒
d	𐎄	ṡ	𐎠
ḏ	𐎏	ʻ	𐎓
h	𐎅	ġ	𐎙
w	𐎆	p	𐎔
z	𐎇	ṣ	𐎕
ḥ	𐎈	q	𐎖
ḫ	𐎃	r	𐎗
ṭ	𐎉	š	𐎘
t̠	𐎑	t	𐎚
y	𐎊	t̠	𐎘

The hypothetical decipherment was regarded as successful because it actually worked: the texts could be read and understood (on the basis of comparison with other Semitic languages) and they proved to include extremely important myths, rituals and administrative documents. However, the decipherment received its definitive seal of certainty when in 1955 a new tablet was found at Ugarit which, though it was broken, listed the majority of the letters and gave alongside each one the consonantal equivalent as represented in the Akkadian cuneiform script (with vowel attached, since the Sumero-Akkadian system cannot express consonants alone).

The remarkable thing about the Ugaritic alphabet, apart from its early date, was the fact that it was a *cuneiform* alphabet. This makes it look superficially like Akkadian

7 The Ugaritic cuneiform alphabet.

cuneiform, but the individual signs are different from the Akkadian signs. No doubt the basic technology of writing followed a Mesopotamian model (Akkadian texts were well known in the West at this time), but the actual forms of the letters seem to have been inspired at least in part by the linear alphabet of the Proto-Canaanite/Proto-Sinaitic inscriptions.

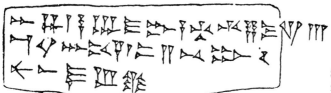

8 Ugaritic abecedary found in 1948.

8 Ugarit also gives us our first glimpse of an established ordering of the letters of the alphabet, since an abecedary text was found in 1948 which simply lists the letters in order: 'a, b, g, ḫ, d, h, w, z, ḥ, ṭ, y, k, š, l, m, ḏ, n, ṯ, s, ʽ, p, ṣ, q, r, ṯ, ġ, t, 'i, 'u, ś. The last three appear to be additional and so we have basically a twenty-seven-letter system which has been expanded by the addition of 'i, 'u and ś, a special s-sound used outside literary texts in words of Hurrian origin and in texts actually *in* Hurrian, since the Ugaritic cuneiform alphabet was also used at Ugarit for this language. This cuneiform alphabet is a 'long' alphabet by comparison with the 'short' twenty-two-letter alphabet used for Phoenician and Hebrew.

The sound represented as ' in transliteration is the glottal stop between two vowels, heard today in Glasgow and Cockney dialects of English in the pronunciation of words such as 'bottle' as /boʼel/, and between the /e/ and the /o/ of modern German *beobachten*. In the Ugaritic script there are three varieties of this letter *aleph* (as it is called in Hebrew). Apparently the two extra forms of *aleph*, 'i and 'u, were devised as aids to help indicate the vowel following the *aleph* (or sometimes in front of it), though without any distinction in vowel length. Occasionally these signs seem to be used as pure vowel signs without the glottal stop, though this is not normal. It is best to regard the emergence of the three *aleph*s as an intrusion of syllabic writing into an otherwise consonantal system. The Ugaritic scribes who developed the long cuneiform alphabet may have been inspired in this regard by the existence of certain syllabic cuneiform signs which were sometimes used simply to indicate a vowel. The Ugaritic forms of 'i and 'u may actually be derived from the Akkadian signs for i and ú. Like the letter ś, they may have been devised especially to assist with the writing of non-Semitic words.

There are other cuneiform alphabetic inscriptions of similar date, perhaps a little later, from the area to the south of Ugarit. These appear at various sites including Taʽanach, Nahal Tavor and Beth Šemeš in Palestine, Tell Nebi Mend in Syria and Sarepta in Lebanon. There is even an inscription from Cyprus (Hala Sultan Tekke), though the silver dish on which it is found may be an import from the Levantine coast.

Some of these other inscriptions, as well as a small number of texts from Ugarit itself, are in the shorter alphabet. This shorter repertoire was more or less adequate for the later languages of the area, such as Phoenician and Hebrew, though it may be noted that at least one of the Hebrew letters was pronounced in two different ways which later had to be distinguished by the use of additional marks (on this see below). Indeed one of the inscriptions in alphabetic cuneiform, the one from Sarepta in Lebanon, seems to be in the Phoenician language.

It is not easy to explain the complex history of the alphabet in this period. According to a widespread view, the alphabet was being shortened because linguistic changes were taking place which involved the loss of certain sounds. Thus Hebrew did not need to represent /ḫ/, /t̠/, /t̪/, /ġ/ or /t̠/, while /š/ *was* needed, but came to be represented by the otherwise unwanted sign for /t̠/, so that the old letter š was dropped. The shorter cuneiform alphabet is usually seen as a step in this direction. At the same time the sporadic nature of the finds has been taken to suggest that the idea of a cuneiform alphabet did not really catch on and become popular. It is essentially medium-related and depends upon the local availability of suitable clay. More importantly, the southern area of Syria/Palestine was under considerable Egyptian influence at this time and it appears that writing, using a descendant of the Proto-Sinaitic/ Proto-Canaanite script, was normally done on papyrus, which rarely survives in this area.

Recently another theory has been put forward which, while attractive, as yet lacks sufficient proof. It is, however, worthy of being recorded here. There is some evidence to support the view that the Ugaritic alphabet is an expanded version of the shorter cuneiform alphabet which must, therefore, have preceded it, rather than a longer prototype of the later shortened alphabet. On this view there would have been in the area of Syria/Palestine in the middle of the second millennium BC two alphabets, a linear one and a cuneiform one, side by side. The cuneiform version was widespread but much less used. It was expanded to allow for extra sounds which were needed as a result of southern Semitic – Arabian – influence. The Ugaritic language has a full range of consonantal sounds, as do South Arabian and the much later Arabic. There are other signs of an Arabian connection in Ugaritic culture.

A key piece of evidence would be the cuneiform alphabetic text from Beth Šemeš, which is in fact an abecedary, though instead of following the established West Semitic order (beginning ', b, g, d ...), it follows the South Arabian order (h, l, ḥ, m ...). (On letter-ordering, see the next section.) This would suggest that what we know as the South Arabian letter-order (though only from a later date) intruded into Palestine, perhaps with an incoming ethnic group, at a very early date. However, there is much that is unproved in this neat schema.

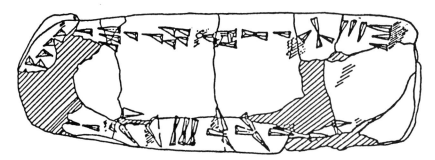

9 The Beth Šemeš abecedary: cuneiform alphabet with South Arabian letter-order.

The Ugaritic cuneiform is the only well-known alphabetic cuneiform. There is no doubt that the cuneiform alphabets disappeared and the other branch of alphabetic tradition, that of the forms descended from the Proto-Sinaitic/Proto-Canaanite script, replaced it. Ugarit itself was destroyed by the Sea Peoples *c.* 1200 BC, and with it disappeared the Ugaritic alphabet.

Direction of Writing and Abecedaries
Since the cuneiform alphabets give us our first coherent evidence on the subject, it is appropriate here to add some comments on the direction of writing and on the ordering of letters to form the complete alphabet.

West Semitic texts before the emergence of the Phoenician script are not uniform in their direction of writing. The Ugaritic alphabet is written from left to right like classical Greek, Latin and English, but there are a few Ugaritic texts which follow the opposite pattern, right to left. The earlier Proto-Sinaitic/Proto-Canaanite scripts are very irregular: writing could be in either direction or vertical. Some early Greek and South Arabian texts are written boustrophedon (βουστροφηδόν) – like an ox ploughing a field: from left to right in the first line, right to left in the second, left to right in the third and so on (or starting on the right in the first line). In such inscriptions the letters are often reversed to face the direction of writing.

With the settling down of the Phoenician alphabet *c.* 1100–1050 BC, the right-to-left order became fixed and so it has remained for the main Semitic scripts which survive to the present day. It may be noted that this fact is of some significance in the discussion of the date at which the Greeks received the alphabet from the Phoenicians, since in the earliest Greek inscriptions the direction is still *not* fixed (see below).

The ordering of the alphabet is best established from abecedaries, school or practice texts in which a trainee lists the letters of the alphabet in the order in which he has learnt them. The complete Ugaritic abecedary, referred to earlier, clearly established the Ugaritic letter-order. This order is interesting not only in itself but, as we have seen, because of what it reveals about the development of the Ugaritic alphabet. It seems that the three letters at the end, 'i, 'u, ṡ, were added at a secondary stage of development. Apparently 'i and 'u, the additional forms of the letter 'a, were added at the end before ṡ was finally attached. This avoided disrupting the traditional order.

The ordering of the Phoenician and Hebrew alphabets is the same as that of the basic Ugaritic twenty-seven-letter alphabet, after the removal of ḫ, š (replaced by the sign formerly used for /t/), ḏ, ṯ and ġ: ʾ, b, g, d, h, w, z, ḥ, ṭ, y, k, l, m, n, s, ʿ, p, ṣ, q, r, š (old ṯ), t. Hence Ugarit's claim to have established the first alphabet so far known to history, though as we have seen, its is not the first alphabetic writing. Reference to another major traditional Semitic letter-ordering pattern is found in the next section.

Also of interest are the names of the letters. Many of these correspond to the object depicted in the original pictograph from which the letter developed. Thus the letter **b** is called *bēt* in Hebrew, i.e. 'house', and the original pictograph was a picture of a house. These names go back to the very beginnings of the alphabet. Letters added later tended not to have proper names of this kind, while the names for the original letters were fixed to such a degree that when the Greeks took over the Phoenician alphabet (see below) they retained the old names, *alpha, bēta* (ἄλφα, βῆτα) etc., despite the fact that the names were absolutely meaningless in Greek.

The South Arabian Alphabet

Directly related to the linear proto-alphabet is the alphabetic system adopted in southern Arabia. The inscriptions in this script come from ancient South Arabian kingdoms such as those of the Sabaeans and the Minaeans, and the earliest may date to *c.* 500 BC or earlier, though the script did not die out until *c.* AD 600. Despite all efforts, these inscriptions are notoriously difficult to date.

10

It is thought that another small group of inscriptions represents the link between the Proto-Canaanite and the South Arabian scripts. These come not from southern Arabia but from Babylonia (seventh century BC) and from near Elath on the Gulf of Aqaba (eighth to seventh centuries BC). There are also

10 South Arabian inscription from Saba, 2nd century BC. BM WA 103021

other inscriptions of an intermediary type from Arabia. These materials are called Proto-Arabian and this Proto-Arabian script seems to have branched off from Proto-Canaanite *c*. 1300 BC.

In the north of Arabia there are also well-known relatives of the South Arabian script, more or less contemporary with it, including the scripts used for such languages as Lihyanite, Thamudic and Safaitic. The dating of these texts is again difficult. They probably run from several centuries BC right down to the Islamic period. One precisely dated example in this category of script is a bilingual in Thamudic script and Nabataean script (though the *language* of the Nabataean part seems in fact to be early Arabic). The Nabataean text contains a date which fixes the text at AD 267–8.

An offshoot of this script was exported to Ethiopia and forms the basis of the classical Ethiopic (Ge'ez) and modern Amharic scripts (see below). The first Ge'ez inscriptions were actually written in the monumental South Arabian script.

11   By careful reconstruction of rather fragmentary evidence, it has been concluded that the order of the twenty-nine South Arabian letters was as follows: **h, l, ḥ, m, q, w, š, r, b** (or **ġ**), **t, s, k, n, ḫ, ś, f, ', ', ḍ, g, d, ġ** (or **b**), **ṭ, z, ḏ, y, ṯ, ṣ/ẓ.** As has been noted above, it has been discovered recently that the ordering of the alphabet in southern Arabia has a precedent in one of the cuneiform alphabetic texts *not* from Ugarit, i.e. the Beth Šemeš tablet, which gives the alphabet in the South Arabian order. It is therefore likely that the South Arabian alphabetic tradition goes right back into the second millennium BC.

Y	h	✗	s	⋈	ḍ
٦	l	↑	k	⊓	ġ
Ψ	ḥ	⌐	n	▥	ṭ
◁	m	Y	ḫ	✗	z
◊	q	⋛	ś	Η	ḏ
⊕	w	◊	f	٩	y
⼍	š	⼍	'	৪	ṯ
)	r	○	'	𝓡	ṣ
Π	b	⊟	ḍ	𝓡	ẓ
Χ	t	⌐	g		

11 The South Arabian alphabet.

3

Consolidation of the Alphabet and Export to the West

Although the main evidence of the Proto-Sinaitic/Proto-Canaanite and even cuneiform alphabets is in the south – Palestine, Sinai, etc., with Ugarit an outpost of the cuneiform alphabet in the north – some early and much later evidence suggests that the Phoenician coast and specifically Byblos may have been a major focus of script development.

The Phoenician, Hebrew and Aramaic Alphabets
The twenty-two-letter Byblian alphabet (the Phoenician alphabet) evolved *c.* 1050 BC in a direct line of descent from the earlier linear alphabets. As we have seen, the right-to-left orientation of writing and the stylised linear character of the letters became fixed at about this time. The inscription of the Ahiram sarcophagus, dated *c.* 1000 BC, finds the script already in a classic 12
form. Other inscriptions, also from Byblos, follow soon after.

12 Phoenician inscription of Ahiram. From Byblos, late 11th century BC.

A little later the Phoenician script spread and came to be used by kingdoms to the north, as is evidenced by ninth-century BC inscriptions from Zincirli (Ya'udi/Sam'al) in modern Turkey and from Karatepe (also in Turkey, eighth century BC). The latter are especially important since they are in fact bilingual in Phoenician and Hieroglyphic Hittite.

Within the Phoenician orbit, the script was later used in the so-called Punic colonies of the Phoenicians around the Mediterranean. Other Phoenician mater- 13,14
ials have been found, for example, at Ur in Mesopotamia and in Cyprus. Most of these inscriptions are carved on stone, but a few are in ink and there are some signs of a tendency towards more cursive forms. Phoenician and Punic inscriptions continued to be produced until the second to third centuries AD.

13 Phoenician inscription on obelisk from Kition (Cyprus), 4th century BC. BM WA 125082

14 Phoenician votive inscription from Idalion (Cyprus), 390 BC. BM WA 125315

The Phoenician alphabet spread south to the Hebrews and was adopted by the Aramaeans to the east. Both the Hebrews and the Aramaeans were at this time establishing kingdoms. The Aramaeans have left a number of monumental inscriptions, while the Hebrew material is mostly of a less dramatic kind, though extensive in the quantity (letters, seals, etc.) which has come to light, partly as a result of the intensive archaeological exploration of Palestine.

15   Thus three main West Semitic scripts emerged from the earlier Byblian linear alphabet. The primary one was the Phoenician, from which the Aramaic and Hebrew scripts are usually thought to be derived. The twenty-two-letter Phoenician script, which had become stabilised *c.* 1050 BC, remained essentially unchanged during most of its long life; Phoenician bears the great distinction of having been the probable source used by the Greeks for their adoption of the alphabet.

The Phoenician script was at first used unchanged by the Hebrews, who

	Early Phoenician	Moabite	Hebrew Ostraca (sixth century BC)	Early Aramaic	Late Aramaic Papyri	Palmyrene Aramaic	Monumental Nabataean Aramaic	'Square' Jewish/ Hebrew Printed
ʾ								א
b								ב
g								ג
d								ד
h								ה
w								ו
z								ז
ḥ								ח
ṭ								ט
y								י
k								כ
l								ל
m								מ
n								נ
s								ס
ʿ								ע
p								פ
ṣ								צ
q								ק
r								ר
š								ש
t								ת

15 Phoenician, Hebrew and Aramaic scripts.

30

16 The Hebrew Gezer 'Calendar', 10th century BC.

17 Moabite inscription of King Mesha from Dibon (Jordan), c. 850 BC. Louvre AO 5066

accepted the script along with a whole cluster of other cultural traditions from the peoples they met when they settled in Palestine. Thus the very earliest Hebrew inscription is in the Phoenician script. This is the so-called Gezer Calendar, a small tenth-century BC stone tablet bearing a brief catalogue of the agricultural activities of the year. In fact, it cannot be easily decided linguistically whether this text is actually Hebrew or Phoenician. Surprisingly, the best witness to the earliest distinctively Hebrew script-form is the ninth-century BC Moabite inscription of King Mesha, the Moabites having used the Hebrew script. Y. Aharoni, it may be noted, attempted to identify in a tenth-century BC inscription from Arad a transitional script between the Phoenician and the Hebrew.

However, the Phoenician script was not entirely satisfactory from the Hebrew point of view. Hebrew has some sounds not represented in Phoenician. At least in later periods, one of the letters taken by Hebrew from Phoenician, the letter we transliterate as š, was in fact pronounced in Hebrew in two different ways, as /š/ (i.e. /sh/) and /ś/; the precise manner of articulation of the latter is uncertain, but it was different from the other Hebrew s-sounds and may have resembled the Welsh /ll/ as in llan. Later Hebrew came to distinguish the two by placing a dot on the right or left of the letter. It would have been feasible to invent a new letter, but writing systems are extraordinarily conservative once established and the Phoenician model was dominant. Hence no such radical innovation was undertaken.

18 Hebrew tomb inscription from Jerusalem, 8th–7th century BC. BM WA 125205

19 Hebrew ostracon from Lachish, early 6th century BC. BM WA 125702

Other Hebrew inscriptions follow in a long series throughout the first millennium BC. These include, for example, the inscription of the royal steward Shebaniah from Siloam (eighth to seventh centuries BC) and ostraca from Samaria (eighth century), Arad (seventh to sixth centuries), Yavneh-Yam (seventh century) and Lachish (sixth century). There are also clay sealings, *bullae*, from Lachish, Arad and Jerusalem, which were originally attached to papyrus documents. These show the importance of the writing of Hebrew on papyrus at this period, though sadly virtually all of it has perished.

Politically and culturally, ancient Israel was somewhat isolated and as a result the developments in the script during this long period are limited. There are certain tendencies to a more cursive style, but almost all our sources are inscribed on stone and pot and we have very little information about writing on soft materials. A good example of a stone inscription is the Siloam tunnel

20 Hebrew inscription from the Siloam tunnel, Jerusalem, c. 700 BC.

inscription (eighth century BC), which is probably meant to be a formal monumental inscription but actually contains many cursive features, with downstrokes curving to the left. The cursive form seems to have been normal and there may have been no Hebrew tradition of royal inscriptions requiring a monumental script.

The Hebrew script, having been in decline from the time of the Babylonian exile (sixth century BC), when Aramaic was in the ascendant, was eventually abandoned by the Jewish community in favour of the Aramaic script. The old script, called in later Jewish tradition $k^e tāb$ 'ibrī, 'Hebrew script', did not, however, disappear immediately. Among the Dead Sea Scrolls there are Bible fragments in the old script (Leviticus) and there are also coins from the Hasmonaean period (135–37 BC) and the first and second Jewish Revolts AD 66–70 and 132–5 bearing legends written in it. The retention of the old script may have had an element of nationalism about it. It was also favoured by certain Jewish sects, certainly by the Samaritans, who retained it throughout the ages. By contrast, the orthodox tradition of mainstream rabbinic Judaism came to be rather hostile to the old script and gave legitimacy to the newly adopted Aramaic script by ascribing its introduction to Ezra who, it was claimed, brought it with him on

21 Samaritan Bible manuscript (Gen 21: 4–14), 13th century AD. Chester Beatty Library (Dublin) Ms 751 27v

the return from exile in Babylon. According to the Mishnah, a collection of Jewish legal judgements compiled *c.* AD 200, the Law scroll (Torah), when written in the old Hebrew script (as it was by the Samaritans), did not have about it the same sanctity as adhered to a normal scroll in the Jewish Aramaic script.

The Aramaic script, derived from the Phoenician in about the eleventh to tenth centuries BC, was the most vibrant of the three scripts. Not only did it ultimately supplant the other two, it also spread far beyond the area of the Aramaean people and became a script of convenience for Assyrians, Persians and others and was used in Egypt, Arabia, Cilicia, Anatolia, Afghanistan, etc. At first Aramaic basically used the Phoenician script, as evidenced by Aramaic inscriptions from Zincirli, Hamath and Damascus in the ninth to eighth centuries BC. But, as a result of its international currency under the Assyrians and the powers which succeeded them, it developed extremely rapidly, diverging from Phoenician from the eighth century BC onwards and becoming increasingly cursive and more and more simplified. The Aramaic language

22

22 Aramaic inscription on stele of King Zakkur of Hamath, *c.* 780–775 BC. Louvre AO 8185

23 Aramaic funerary stele from Neirab (Syria), 7th century BC. Louvre AO 3027

24 Aramaic papyrus from Elephantine (Egypt), 5th century BC. BL Or Pap cvi AB

and a rather cursive form of the script were used, for example, by Adon, the king of a city-state in Phoenicia in *c.* 600 BC in his letter, fortunately preserved on papyrus, to the Pharaoh. Gradually a difference between formal and cursive styles developed. The cursive is better known and is attested mainly on

24

papyrus and leather from Egypt (sixth to third centuries BC), including papyri from Hermopolis and Elephantine and the Arsham documents, and from Wadi Daliyeh near Jericho (fourth-century BC documents of Samaritan families). However, despite the rapid cursivisation which took place (almost a shorthand developed), the

15

Aramaic script retained, as a result of international use, a virtually complete homogeneity until about a century after the collapse of the Persian Empire, the last cohesive force holding it together.

Again there were sounds which were inadequately represented by the Phoenician script, but no new signs were added. Indeed, to some extent developments in the Aramaic language, such as the disappearance of the sounds /d̲/ and /t̲/, relieved the problem of the absence of signs for these.

It is worth noting a recent discovery which could have a profound effect on our perception of the way (outlined in the previous paragraphs) in which the Aramaic script relates to the Phoenician script. This is the long inscription, a bilingual in Aramaic and in Assyrian cuneiform, from Tell Fakhariyah (ancient Sikanu) found in 1979 near Tell Halaf in north-east Syria. The date of this inscription, while not precisely known, is certainly not earlier than the ninth century BC, yet the script is peculiar by comparison with other, slightly later, Aramaic inscriptions which are probably more strongly under Phoenician influence. Awareness of this influence is the basis of the traditional view outlined above, that the Aramaic script derived from the Phoenician.

However, some of the peculiarities of script of the new inscription are shared with earlier forms of the linear script. For example, the letter 'ayin appears with a dot in the centre: ⊙. The dot had disappeared from the Phoenician form of 'ayin much earlier. Therefore, it is possible that there existed in the East an early offshoot of the Proto-Canaanite script which developed independently before being replaced by the more dominant script-form of the Aramaic of the West. At the time of writing, however, this view has not yet found wide acceptance – it is quite revolutionary and will take some time to evaluate.

There are other minor scripts worth noting which are derived from Phoenician either directly or via Hebrew or Aramaic. The Moabite script, attested

principally in the Mesha inscription of *c.* 850 BC, derives from Hebrew (though   17
it predates most of our evidence for Hebrew). It was used in central Jordan,
south of Amman. By the sixth century BC it had come under Aramaic influence.
The Ammonite script further north (around Amman) may derive from Aramaic
(the Aramaic of Damascus) or show strong Aramaic influence. The evidence
of an Edomite script tradition in southern Jordan is meagre. Edomite is represented in the seventh to sixth centuries BC by seals, weights, fragmentary ostraca
and fragmentary writings on stone. L. G. Herr identified a southern Palestinian/
Transjordanian grouping of scripts, including Moabite and Edomite with
Hebrew, while J. Naveh emphasises the Aramaic influence on the Edomite
script (from the seventh century BC onwards). There is virtually no evidence
of a Philistine script and none of these minor scripts had any long-term significance.

Gradually, then, from as early as the ninth to eighth centuries BC, the Phoenician, Hebrew and Aramaic scripts had begun to diverge to some extent, forming   15
national script-traditions, though the Aramaic one would have to be called
an international rather than a national script.

Finally, before moving on, we may note one other feature, the use initially
by Aramaic and then also by Hebrew (and the minor scripts) of vowel-letters,
i.e. the occasional use of certain consonants, particularly **h, w** and **y**, to represent
vowels. Aramaic from an early date used them for vowels within words as
well as at the end of words. Hebrew at first used them only at the ends of
words, but gradually extended this use to the internal vowels. Thus the Hebrew
h could stand for /o/, /a/ or /e/ at the end of a word. The letters **w** and
y were typically used to represent /u/ and /i/, normally /ū/ and /ī/. Not all
the vowels could be represented in this way even when the system, which
was never used totally consistently, was fully operational, but this development
does show that the lack of vowels was seen as a problem.

The Export of the Alphabet to Greece

There is a widely accepted view that the Greeks learned the alphabet from
the peoples of the Phoenician coast (see B.F. Cook, *Greek Inscriptions*, pp.
8–11). This can be clearly demonstrated by a comparison of the Phoenician
and early Greek letters. Some of the letters – **A** is a good example – even
retain an element of the pictograph, in this case the drawing of a bull's head
(∀), now upside down and without eyes! The Greek name for this letter
is *alpha* (ἄλφα), a word which is meaningless in Greek (apart from referring
to this particular letter) but which means 'bull' in West Semitic languages
(e.g. Ugaritic *'alpu*, Hebrew *'elef*). This is true of almost all the Greek letter-
names. The letter-order in Phoenician and Greek is basically the same, though
some supplementary letters were developed and added to the alphabetic order:
Υ, Φ, Χ, Ψ, Ω. The ascription of the alphabet to the Phoenicians was firmly
embedded in Greek historical tradition as found in the works of the fifth-century

BC Greek historian Herodotus. The letters are called *phoinikeia grammata* (Φοινιχήια Γράμματα), 'Phoenician letters', and were supposed to have been brought to Greece by the legendary Kadmos.

Much less certain are the date and the route of the transmission of the alphabet to the Greeks. The arguments are complex. On the question of date, we should first note the *varieties* of the earliest Greek script, which is first known to us in the eighth century BC. Forms of letters vary considerably and the earliest Greek inscriptions are sometimes written from left to right, sometimes right to left and sometimes boustrophedon (see p. 24). On the other hand, the similarities between the Greek scripts, including the use of certain letters to represent vowels (below), clearly indicate a single common origin. The need to allow time for the diversification of the Greek scripts suggests a date for the import of the alphabet well before the eighth century BC.

25,26,27

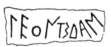

25 Early Greek inscriptions from Athens and Thera.

26 Early Greek inscription from Ephesus, 6th century BC. BM GR 1867. 11–12. 441

Early Greek Alphabets: 8th–7th centuries BC					
Athens	Thera	Crete	Naxos	Corcyra	Boeotia

(chart of early Greek letterforms by region)

27 Early Greek alphabets, 8th–7th centuries BC.

Further, it can be argued that certain of the forms of letters taken over by the Greeks, for example the short o with a dot in it ($\odot$) reflecting the pictograph of an eye (the corresponding Semitic letter is called 'ayin, meaning 'eye'), are quite early forms, also indicating a very early date. Again, by the eighth century BC, the right-to-left direction of writing was already the rule in the scripts derived from Phoenician, so that it is hard to imagine the Greeks borrowing the script at that late date and still being uncertain on direction. The likeliest earlier date would be c. 1100–1050 BC. Against this, however, we have to place the fact that at the moment our earliest Greek evidence is of *c.* 740–730 BC. Further, some of the evidence may be uncertain; as we have seen, the supposedly very early dotted o is now found in an Aramaic inscription of the ninth century BC. Hence suggestions of an earlier date for the Greek alphabet remain speculative and are a matter of heated debate among scholars.

As to the route by which the alphabet passed to the Greeks, there is almost universal agreement that Phoenicia was the starting point. We have seen that native Greek tradition supposed this. There is, however, room for debate about where the encounter with the Phoenician alphabet took place. It need not have been in mainland Greece and the context may well have been commercial activity. The point of contact might have been in the Ugaritic region, since there were Greek settlements there in the late ninth century BC (e.g. Tell Sukas), though we may note also the occurrence of Phoenician inscriptions in Cyprus and Sardinia. But much of this is speculation and we cannot absolutely exclude another possible route. We have seen that there is evidence in the ninth century BC of an independent, eastern Aramaic script-tradition with affinities with early Greek script. Further, the names of many of the Greek letters (*alpha, bēta, gamma, delta*) have an /-a/ suffix which is a distinctive feature of Aramaic of all types (though it could have other explanations in these Greek letter-names). North-east Syria, the Aramaean homeland, had its own routes of contact with the Greek world which ran through Anatolia and did not involve Phoenicia. This could be a source for the early Greek script and would eliminate some of the arguments for an eleventh-century borrowing of the script, bringing us back to the traditional date of the ninth or eighth centuries BC.

Although the Greeks basically played a secondary role to the western Semitic peoples, they added a new dimension to alphabetic writing. A number of the Phoenician letters which were not needed for consonants in particular Greek dialects were put to use to represent vowels. The Phoenician letter ʿ*ayin*, written as a circle and representing a guttural not found in Greek, came to be used for the vowel /o/. The Phoenician letter *he* ultimately came to be used for /e/ (**E**) and *yod* for /i/ (**I**). Similarly, the sign for the glottal stop, *aleph* (ʾ), was used as **A**. The sign for fricative (dotted) /ḥ/ (pronounced as a roughly breathed aitch, as in a stage whisper) came to be used for /ē/ as Greek **H**. Another originally Phoenician sign was adapted for use as /u/ü/, the latter as in German *über*, French *sur* (Greek **Y**), and finally ordinary **O** was modified by being opened at the bottom to produce **Ω**, long /ō/. Some of these developments were at first confined to the Ionic dialect of Greek, but eventually they spread and Greek had letters to represent /a/, /e/, /ē/, /i/, /o/, /ō/ and /u/ü/ (**A, E, H, I, O, Ω, Y**): a full range of essential vowels. This meant that a true alphabet was for the first time in operation, an alphabet in which not only consonants but vowels too were represented. This was, of course, an enormous advance on the Phoenician and other Semitic systems, though, as we have seen, certain consonant-signs (especially in Aramaic) *were* adapted for use also as vowels. The Semitic scripts eventually introduced alphabetic vowel-notation by adding signs above and below the consonants. One of the Syriac scripts, ironically, made the transition to representing vowels by re-importing the Greek vowel-signs and adding them above and below the line!

Greek also invented, in addition to the sign for /ō/ (Ω), special signs for /ph/, /kh/ and /ps/ (Φ, X, Ψ), adding them with Y and Ω to the end of its alphabet.

Some archaic dialects of Greek included letters derived from Phoenician (or Proto-Canaanite) which did not survive with their original value – for example, *digamma*, pronounced /w/, from Phoenician *wāw*, shaped roughly like our F (and, in fact, the source of our F). There seem to have been eastern and western variants of the Greek alphabet. The most important eastern variant was the Ionic form, including various other scripts of Asia Minor and eastern Greece. An example of the variation is the different treatment of the signs for Phoenician /h/ and /ḥ/. In the East these were used for /e/ and /ē/ (Greek E and H), but in the West the Phoenician H was used for both /e/ and /ē/, while the Phoenician Ḥ was used for a breathy version of aitch – a sound similar to its original Phoenician sound. After several twists and turns of development, the Ionic alphabet of Miletus was officially adopted in Athens in 403/2 BC and comes to us as the 'classical' Greek alphabet, in which the direction of writing – left to right – had become invariable. The other, variant, alphabets gradually died out. The classical Greek alphabet runs as follows: A, B, Γ, Δ, E, Z, H, Θ, I, K, Λ, M, N, Ξ, O, Π, P, Σ, T, Y, Φ, X, Ψ, Ω (i.e. A, B, G, D, E, Z, Ē, Th, I, K, L, M, N, Ks, O, P, R, S, T, U, Ü, Ph, Kh, Ps, Ō).

A number of offshoots of the Greek alphabet developed for other languages, and such offshoots had to adapt to the repertoires of sounds used in those languages. We may note Lycian (in southern Asia Minor), Coptic (in Egypt) and Etruscan (in Italy, where there were Greek colonies, for example, on the island of Pithecusa from *c.* 775 BC). Etruscan inscriptions are found from very early on; the Etruscans must have received the alphabet in about the eighth century BC. The Etruscan alphabet at first had twenty-six letters (written from right to left or boustrophedon), perhaps borrowed from Greek colonists from Chalcis in Euboea, though this number had been reduced by the end of the fifth century BC to a standard form representing twenty letters: /a/, /e/, /i/, /u/, /g~k/, /v/ (i.e. *digamma*), /z/, /h/, /th/, /l/, /m/, /n/, /p/, *san* (an extra s derived ultimately from Phoenician), /r/, /s/, /t/, /ph/, /kh/, /f/. The latest dated Etruscan inscription comes from the first century AD; the Etruscan script was completely superseded, one could say swamped, by the Latin script as it spread with the Roman Empire. It is possible that the Etruscan script is the ancestor of the various runic scripts of northern Europe.

Other later derivatives of the Greek script (with some Latin elements) may be noted, particularly the Cyrillic script (ninth century AD) and its associated scripts used for various Slavic languages. Other Slavs, including the Poles and the Czechs, were to adopt the Latin script with modifications. For further discussion of these important scripts see D. Diringer, *Writing*, pp. 156 ff.

The Latin Alphabet

Our own alphabet is, of course, derived – though not directly – from that of the Greeks. The mediators were the Etruscans, whose script was transmitted to the Romans. The Roman or Latin script (Latin being the name of the Romans' language) is very similar to our own, apart from certain minor modifications introduced in the Middle Ages. Early Latin inscriptions go back to the seventh to sixth centuries BC, a date at which the direction of writing was still from right to left (or even boustrophedon as in the early Greek inscriptions).

The procedure of transmission to the Romans was complex but can be explained as follows (note that capitals or upper-case letters are used consistently in this section to refer to letter-forms, and small or lower-case letters between slashes to refer to sounds, as the lower-case Latin forms did not actually emerge until later).

The Etruscans had no distinct /g/ sound and used the G-sign (like a modern C) for /k/. The old K-sign thus ceased to be of use, being replaced by C (pronounced as in 'cat'), and it was basically without any K that the alphabet came to the Romans, though for obscure reasons they did retain K for a very few specific words. The Romans, unlike the Etruscans, *did* need to represent /g/ and, since the old G-sign had already been used to represent /k/, which they also needed, they invented a new sign for /g/ by adding a stroke to the existing C, thereby producing G. In the letter-order it took the place of the Greek Z, which was not essential for Latin, though Z was secondarily reintroduced into the Latin alphabet to help with the writing of words of Greek origin and thus came to stand at the end of the alphabet. The Romans did not need to represent /th/ or /ks/ (Θ, Ξ), or the sounds /ph/, /kh/, /ps/ and /ō/, for which Greek had added letters at the end of the alphabet (Φ, in practice replaced by F, a derivative of the archaic Greek *digamma* and ultimately derived from Phoenician *wāw*, X, Ψ and Ω). They did need to represent /u/ü/, Greek Y, which, in the form of V, was used for both /v/ and /u/, while I stood for /i/ and the consonant /y/. At a secondary stage Y was reintroduced as a separate letter, like Z, though added to the letter-order before Z. It, too, was used in words of Greek origin. Thus the Roman alphabet was as follows: A, B, C (=/k/), D, E, F, G, H, I, K, L, M, N, O, P, Q (derived from an archaic Greek letter), R (originally in its Greek form P, identical with the sign we use for /p/), S, T, V, X (a derivative of Greek Ξ /ks/, not the Greek X [/kh/]), Y, Z. Other differences between the Greek and Latin scripts (e.g. in the forms of Latin D *v.* Greek Δ, C/G *v.* Γ, L *v.* Λ and S *v.* Σ) are explained by the fact that the Latin forms are western variants transmitted via Euboean colonies. Much later, in the Middle Ages, U was distinguished from V and consonantal **J** from **I**, and finally, in the eleventh century AD, **W** (double-U) came into existence, though it is still not used in all European languages. It is pronounced as /v/ in German, while the German **V** normally stands for /f/.

From the Latin alphabet came all the western European scripts. Gradually a distinction developed between different styles of writing, notably between upper-case and lower-case letters, also called majuscules and minuscules; the latter were particularly characteristic of normal handwriting. In the Middle Ages, *national* handwriting styles developed. What we call 'Italic' is one of these. In Britain and Ireland there developed the Anglian/Irish script characteristic of some of the great monastic manuscripts of the Middle Ages such as the Book of Kells (*c*. AD 800). The Irish national script has been abandoned relatively recently, as has the 'Gothic' script formerly used by German printers. As we have noted, some of the eastern European peoples adopted a modified form of the Greek script (Russian, etc.). Others have used a version of the Latin script modified by the use of special 'accents', as in č, ł, ø.

A relatively modern case of adaptation is that of Turkish. Ottoman Turkish used the Arabic alphabet for the Turkish language, which is totally unrelated structurally to Arabic despite strong cultural links through Islam and many Arabic loan-words into Turkish. In 1928, as part of a Europeanisation programme, Atatürk replaced the Arabic script with the Latin script, modified by the addition of the following: ç/Ç (/ch/), ğ/Ğ (soft /g/y/), i/İ, ı/I (neutral short vowel similar to the second vowel of 'cousin'), ö/Ö (as in German), ş/Ş (/sh/), ü/Ü (also as in German); c/C is used for /j/ as in 'jam'.

4
Alphabetic Scripts in the Late Antique Middle East

From the eighth century BC onwards, the newly developed alphabet had considerable success not only among the Greeks but also with the Assyrians, the Babylonians and then the Persians. This success is closely bound up with the importance of the Aramaic language, which became a *lingua franca* for diplomacy and trade. Aramaic and the Aramaic variety of the alphabet were thus dispersed over a wide area from Egypt to northern India. As in the case of Greek, non-Semitic languages made use of the alphabet.

It may have been under the inspiration of the Aramaic alphabet that the Persians attempted to invent a cuneiform alphabet for Old Persian, though all that was achieved was a much simplified syllabic script.

We have seen that Aramaic was used as an official language by the Assyrians, Babylonians and Persians. After the collapse of the Persian Empire, the Imperial Aramaic language and script, which had been more or less unified across the Empire, began to break up, and local dialects and scripts developed. The main local variants were Jewish, Nabataean, Palmyrene, Hatran and Syriac. In addition there is the Mandaic script, which is attested later but actually goes back to a script contemporary with those already mentioned. It may be noted, although there is no need to go into the details, that the increasing use of joined-up, cursive forms in some of these scripts – the Jewish script, the Syriac and the Nabataean (along with Arabic, derived from the same script tradition) – led, first, to the emergence of 'final' forms of letters (i.e. forms taken by particular letters at the end of a word, resulting basically from the fact that there was no need to join up with what followed), and, second, to the development of special conventions about *how* to make joins, if any, on the right and left of each letter.

The so-called Jewish script is the form of the western Aramaic script which developed in Palestine in the service of the Jewish community. At first it existed alongside the Hebrew script, which was a continuation of the old Hebrew script discussed earlier. Gradually, however, the old Hebrew script fell into general disuse and the Aramaic script began to be used even for writing the Hebrew language. It was used for manuscripts of the Hebrew Bible from as early as the third century BC (Dead Sea Scrolls text of the Book of Exodus). In the inter-testamental period, the majority of the Dead Sea Scrolls texts are in this script, which is also attested in early papyri (e.g. the Nash papyrus of the second century BC) and inscriptions, some in mosaic, including synagogue inscriptions.

28 Jewish (Square Hebrew) script: Pentateuch with Tiberian vowel signs, early 10th century AD. BL Or 4445 f98r

The early history of the script can be divided into three phases: Old Jewish (250–150 BC); Hasmonaean (after the Hasmonaean dynasty, 150–30 BC); and Herodian (30 BC – AD 70). Spread throughout the Jewish diaspora, this newly adopted script in due course became the so-called square script – in Hebrew $k^e t\bar{a}b\ m^e rubb\bar{a}$', 'square script', or $k^e t\bar{a}b$ '$a\check{s}\check{s}\bar{u}r\bar{\imath}$, 'Assyrian script', referring to its approximate place of origin – the standard Jewish book-hand used for all formal purposes. The modern printed forms are as follows (right to left):

א ב ג ד ה ו ז ח ט י כ ל מ נ ס ע פ צ ק ר ש ת

' b g d h w z ḥ ṭ y k l m n s ' p ṣ q r š t

This is known today, somewhat inaccurately, as the Hebrew script. It was used even for Babylonian Jewish Aramaic (i.e. an Aramaic script adopted for Hebrew, naturalised as the 'Hebrew' script and then used once more for Aramaic!). Throughout the Middle Ages it was the standard form of the Jewish/Hebrew script. Alongside there developed a cursive hand, one version of which is seen in the Rashi script (associated with the scholar of that name who died in AD 1105), while another ultimately produced the modern Hebrew cursive.

At a rather uncertain date, probably from the fifth to sixth centuries AD, to which time belong some of the materials recovered at the end of the last century from a Cairo synagogue, Hebrew began to develop systems for adding the vowels and other signs to the consonantal alphabetic texts. The only mark needed to distinguish confusable consonants was that used to distinguish /ś/ and /š/, which for centuries used the same sign. A dot was placed on the left above the letter to indicate /ś/ and a dot on the right to indicate /š/.

(Some earlier traditions use a dot within the letter, or a second small š -sign above the letter, to indicate pronunciation of the sign as /š/, with a small s to indicate pronunciation as /ś/.) Other dots were used (as in Syriac, below) to distinguish variations in pronunciation of certain consonants, notably b, g, d, k, p, t, which could in certain circumstances be pronounced as 'aspirates' (/p/ > /ph/, /t/ > /th/, etc.), and also to indicate doubling of consonants (which is not properly indicated in any of the scripts we have dealt with thus far).

For vowels, the problem was much greater. Earlier, the consonants w, y, h and, to a certain extent, ' had sometimes been used to represent vowels rather than consonants; but now, especially in view of the decline of the Hebrew language and consequent uncertainties about correct pronunciation (particularly of vowels), scholars began to add marks to the text – in the first place to the Biblical text – to clarify the pronunciation. Several systems emerged. The Jewish community in Mesopotamia during the fifth to sixth centuries AD, probably influenced by the use of dots for this purpose in Nestorian Syriac (see below), developed a system of supralinear marks, i.e. marks placed above the line of consonants. This is called the Babylonian system. In Palestine, an earlier so-called Palestinian system gave way in the eighth to ninth centuries AD to a complex and fairly comprehensive system of supralinear and sublinear dots and strokes representing a rather elaborate series of distinctions between vowels. This is the Tiberian system, which subsequently became totally dominant and is used in the later manuscript tradition, especially of Biblical texts.

28

The other major western script form is that of the Nabataeans, the people of the Arab kingdom of Petra, which flourished in the first century BC and the first century AD. The Arab peoples of the area had been using a northern version of the South Arabian script for some time, but the Nabataeans used the Aramaic language and script for public purposes from the fourth century BC onwards. Most of the formal inscriptions come from Petra in Jordan, Madā'in Ṣāliḥ, the Nabataean outpost in Saudi Arabia, and southern Syria, though there are a few from as far afield as Rome, where there was a Nabataean merchant colony. The dates of the main inscriptions, many of them tomb-inscriptions, extend from the second century BC to the annexation of the Nabataean state by the Romans in AD 105–6. Thereafter, literally thousands of short Nabataean inscriptions and graffiti exist, especially from Sinai and southern Jordan/northern Saudi Arabia. Even in formal inscriptions on stone, the Nabataean script is notably cursive in character. Letters are frequently joined

15

29

29 Nabataean formal inscription from Petra, 1st century AD.

and many of the letters have a very rounded shape. A few examples of Nabataean, written in ink on papyrus and on wall-plaster (*c.* AD 100 onwards) have survived. These show that there was a cursive Nabataean alongside the monumental or formal script. (We will return to Nabataean in connection with Arabic.)

In the East, a whole variety of Aramaic scripts developed. The interrelation between these is a matter of dispute. J. Naveh would trace their origin back to an ancestor in the Seleucid period (*c.* 300 BC onwards).

Palmyrene is the very widely attested Aramaic dialect and script of Palmyra/Tadmūr in the Syrian desert. The texts date from the mid-first century BC to the destruction of Palmyra by the Romans in AD 272. Palmyra in the Roman period was a major trading centre; the longest of the Palmyrene texts, a bilingual in Palmyrene Aramaic and Greek, is a taxation tariff. Trade connections took the Palmyrene script to other places, some not far away, such as Dura Europos on the Euphrates, but others at a great distance. Of particular interest is the

15,30

30 Limestone bust with Palmyrene inscription. Palmyra, late 2nd century AD. BM WA 102612

Palmyrene inscription from South Shields, Roman Arbeia, in the north-east of England, carved on behalf of a Palmyrene merchant for his deceased British wife. It probably dates to the early third century AD.

The Palmyrene script existed in two main varieties, a monumental and a cursive one, though the latter is little known and the evidence mostly from materials found outside Palmyra itself. The Syriac script of Edessa in southern Turkey, dealt with in more detail below, is often regarded as derived from or closely related to the Palmyrene – similarities are found in the following letters: ', b, g, d, w, ḥ, y, k, l, m, n, ', r and t – though a strong case can also be made for connecting Syriac closely with a northern Mesopotamian script-family represented principally in texts from Hatra, a city more or less contemporary with Palmyra in Upper Mesopotamia. The Hatran Aramaic inscriptions (approximately four hundred in number) extend in date from the late first century to the third century AD. Closely related inscriptions have been found at Ashur and in south-east Turkey (second century AD). Hatra was under the influence of the Romans' great eastern rival, the Parthians, and provides a link with more easterly regions which also adopted the Aramaic language and/or script.

A southern Mesopotamian group of scripts is represented by Mandaic, used by the Mandaeans of southern Iraq, a religious community with Gnostic and Jewish-Christian characteristics. The Mandaic script is unique as an Aramaic offshoot in that it took the use of vowel-letters to a logical conclusion: *all* vowels are represented in this way, so that the vowels are incorporated into the main line of writing and no additional markings are needed to indicate their existence. Its basic letter-forms seem to belong to a southern Mesopotamian group of Aramaic scripts. The Mandaic may be related to the Elymaic script (Elymais, Khuzistan, at the head of the Arabian Gulf). The latter is known from coins and rock-inscriptions of the second to third centuries AD. There are, however, strong resemblances also between Mandaic and Nabataean, and it may be suspected that there is some western influence involved. The Mandaean sect, which still survives in southern Iraq, claimed to have come from Palestine, and there is much internal evidence from the Mandaean religious literature to support this claim.

There are Aramaic inscriptions from as far afield as Afghanistan and Pakistan, while the Aramaic script was later used for the writing of various non-Semitic languages such as Middle Iranian (Pahlavi) and Uighūr (which is Turkic). In India, too, offshoots of the Aramaic script developed. We may note the Brahmi script (seventh century BC) from which most of the scripts used in India developed and the Kharoṣṭhī script (fifth century BC). Minor derivatives of the Aramaic script were used for inscriptions found at Nisa in Turkmenistan (Parthian ostraca) and Armazi in Georgia (second century AD). The Armenian and Georgian scripts were created in the fifth century AD and also have an Aramaic origin.

ማቴዎስ፦

በአሙ፡ፈ፡ወስ፡እግዚ፡ልፀ፡ፀወፈሐ፡

ወደቤልፃ፡እግዚ፡እ፡ክ	ወገሠሥ፡ም፡ወለስ፡እፅም፡	ነፀ፡ሰቤሃ፡ወተ፡እሠተ፡
ም፡ይተክሠታ፡እ፡ደ፡ን	እ፡ደ፡ን፡ቲ፡ሆ፡ም፡ቀ፡ወ፡ደ፡	እ፡ደ፡ን፡ቲ፡ሆ፡ም፡ወ፡ር፡ን
ቲ፡ነ፡ወ፡እ፡ም፡ሐ፡ር፡ፅ፡ለ፡እ	ሰ፡ም፡በ፡ክ፡ም፡ሃ፡ደ፡ማ፡ና	ይ፡ክ፡ቤ፡ሃ፡ወ፡ተ፡ለ፡ወ፡ይ፡ቀ
ግ፡ዚ፡እ፡ኢ፡የ፡ሱ፡ክ፡ወ፡መ፡ሐ	ት፡ክ፡ም፡ወ፡እ፡ሚ፡ኖ፡ት፡ክ፡ም፡	----
ር፡ም፡እ፡ግ፡ዚ፡እ፡ኢ፡የ፡ሱ፡ክ	ይ፡ኩ፡ን፡ክ፡ም፡ቀ፡ወ፡በ፡ዚ፡ሃ	✤ ✤ ✤ ✤
		(ሐ፡ዋ፡ር፡ያ፡ት)

31 Ethiopic Gospels (Christ healing two blind men), AD 1664–5. BL Or 510 f51a

While the development of the Aramaic scripts continued, older script forms survived in a very few places and underwent their own developments. As we have seen, the old Hebrew script was for the most part replaced by the Aramaic script, but it did not disappear completely. It survived, right down to the modern period, in use among the Jews' Samaritan neighbours, both for Samaritan Hebrew and for Samaritan Aramaic.   21

A much more important backwater from the point of view of script – no denigration of the culture or literature is implied – is Ethiopia. The classical Ethiopian script is closely connected with the old South Arabian script (above,   31 p. 25), which disappeared from southern Arabia when the Arabic language and script took over. The first Ethiopic inscriptions were written in the monumental South Arabian script. For Ethiopic use, the South Arabian alphabet was first reduced from twenty-nine to twenty-four letters and these were then expanded with new inventions to twenty-six. In addition there are labialised forms of certain letters (q, ḫ, k, g) representing /qu/ (as in 'quick'), /gw/ (as in 'Gwent'), etc. The Ethiopian script, written from left to right, continues in use to the present day, though seven extra letters are used for the modern official language of Ethiopia, which is called Amharic.

The Ethiopian script is unique among the Semitic scripts in that it has adapted a consonantal script by adding extra strokes to each consonant in a more or less regular pattern to indicate the vowel following that consonant. This development took place in about the fourth century AD. In theory, the twenty-six consonants could have markers added to them so as to indicate the following   32

Consonant + Vowel	a	u	i	ā	ē	e/no vowel	o
h	ሀ	ሁ	ሂ	ሃ	ሄ	ህ	ሆ
l	ለ	ሉ	ሊ	ላ	ሌ	ል	ሎ
ḥ	ሐ	ሑ	ሒ	ሓ	ሔ	ሕ	ሖ
m	መ	ሙ	ሚ	ማ	ሜ	ም	ሞ
š	ሠ	ሡ	ሢ	ሣ	ሤ	ሥ	ሦ
r	ረ	ሩ	ሪ	ራ	ሬ	ር	ሮ
s	ሰ	ሱ	ሲ	ሳ	ሴ	ስ	ሶ
q	ቀ	ቁ	ቂ	ቃ	ቄ	ቅ	ቆ
b	በ	ቡ	ቢ	ባ	ቤ	ብ	ቦ
t	ተ	ቱ	ቲ	ታ	ቴ	ት	ቶ
ḫ	ኀ	ኁ	ኂ	ኃ	ኄ	ኅ	ኆ
n	ነ	ኑ	ኒ	ና	ኔ	ን	ኖ
ʾ	አ	ኡ	ኢ	ኣ	ኤ	እ	ኦ
k	ከ	ኩ	ኪ	ካ	ኬ	ክ	ኮ
w	ወ	ዉ	ዊ	ዋ	ዌ	ው	ዎ
ʿ	ዐ	ዑ	ዒ	ዓ	ዔ	ዕ	ዖ
z	ዘ	ዙ	ዚ	ዛ	ዜ	ዝ	ዞ
y	የ	ዩ	ዪ	ያ	ዬ	ይ	ዮ
d	ደ	ዱ	ዲ	ዳ	ዴ	ድ	ዶ
g	ገ	ጉ	ጊ	ጋ	ጌ	ግ	ጎ
ṭ	ጠ	ጡ	ጢ	ጣ	ጤ	ጥ	ጦ
p	ጰ	ጱ	ጲ	ጳ	ጴ	ጵ	ጶ
ṣ	ጸ	ጹ	ጺ	ጻ	ጼ	ጽ	ጾ
ḍ	ፀ	ፁ	ፂ	ፃ	ፄ	ፅ	ፆ
f	ፈ	ፉ	ፊ	ፋ	ፌ	ፍ	ፎ
p	ፐ	ፑ	ፒ	ፓ	ፔ	ፕ	ፖ

32 The Ethiopic alphabet: the 26 basic letters with their vowel-markers.

vowel as /a/, /u/, /i/, /ā/, /ē/, /o/ and /e/ or no vowel, producing 182 different syllables, each consisting of consonant plus vowel. To these are to be added five forms of each of the labialised consonants (i.e. a further twenty syllables). Adding the seven Amharic consonants (multiplied by seven for the vowels), we have a grand total of 251 syllabic signs. The basic characteristic features of the form of each vowel remain just about recognisable, but in practice the vowel-markers came to be incorporated into the form of the consonants in a variety of ways, so that the student of this script really has to learn all 251 forms as if they were a syllabary. As a writing system this is almost as cumbersome as syllabic cuneiform, but the Ethiopic script has survived well and boasts an unrivalled beauty and elegance, despite the fact that the letters are never joined. Like ancient South Arabian (and some northern scripts), it uses a word-separator (in the form of two dots, one above the other).

The alphabetic order of Ethiopic is similar to that of South Arabian (h, l, ḥ, m ...) and the names of the letters, thought until recently to be modern intrusions from the Hebrew tradition, may in fact be very ancient. It can be argued that their form is such as to suggest an origin before 1000 BC, which might bring these names right back to the origins of the alphabet itself.

5
Towards the Arabic Alphabet

Among the various forms of the Aramaic script, one which had particularly widespread success was the local form of the script which developed in Edessa (modern Urfa/Şanlıurfa) in the first centuries AD. It is attested at this early date in a number of short inscriptions. The earliest is dated AD 6 (from Birecik, west of Edessa), while a particularly important and unusual text is a long parchment bill of sale from Dura Europos dated AD 243. In its early stages this script was very similar to Palmyrene, but it quickly developed and then received an unexpected boost from the fact that Edessa (Semitic name 'Urhoy) became the focus of the spread of Christianity in the Semitic-speaking world. As a result, by about AD 200 the Bible was translated into the local Aramaic dialect, which became known as Syriac, and the dissemination of the Syriac Bible and the works of Syriac-speaking and -writing theologians led to the use of the Syriac language and script from Palestine to the ends of the Silk Road. Another epigraphic oddity, like the Palmyrene inscription from South Shields, is the bilingual Chinese and Syriac text from Sian in China!

The early Syriac form of writing, known to us in many superb manuscripts frontispiece from the fifth century AD onwards, is the elegant *estrangelā* script. The word 33 is derived from Greek *strongulos* (στρογγύλος) and means 'rounded'. A rather crude version of this script is found in the very earliest Syriac inscriptions of the first century AD from the area of Edessa. As a result of sectarian strife among the Syriac-speaking Christians, there developed western and eastern script variants called respectively Jacobite (after the supposed founder of the 34 western Syrian church, which the orthodox regarded as heretical) and Nestorian (after the supposed heresy of the eastern Syrians). The correct name of the Jacobite script is *serṭā* or *serṭā pᵉšīṭā*, '(script of) the (simple) character', and it is the most cursive of the three. It emerged in the eighth century AD or a little earlier, the earliest dated manuscript coming from AD 731–2. The Nestorian or East Syrian script developed fully later (twelfth to thirteenth centuries AD), but its features appear as early as the sixth century AD, at which point it is still very similar to *estrangelā*. It continued to bear close resemblance to the *estrangelā* script, which itself enjoyed something of a revival in the tenth century AD.

Note may also be made of two minor varieties of Syriac script, the Melkite, derived from *serṭā* and used by Christians loyal to Constantinople, and that used in Palestine for Christian Palestinian Aramaic. The latter is a crude version of *estrangelā* and rather similar to cursive Palmyrene. The Maronites have traditionally used the *serṭā* script.

All three principal forms of Syriac script – *estrangelā*, Jacobite and Nestorian

33 Esṭrangelā Old Syriac Gospels (John 6.53–64), 5th century AD. BL Add 14451 f49b

34 The Syriac scripts.

	Serṭā	Estrangelā	Nestorian
ʾ			
b			
g			
d			
h			
w			
z			
ḥ			
ṭ			
y			
k			
l			
m			
n			
s			
ʿ			
p			
ṣ			
q			
r			
š			
t			

– are extensively preserved in manuscripts and inscriptions and are still in use today. The earliest dated literary manuscript, showing an already mature calligraphic *esṭrangelā* hand, is dated AD 411.

There are two important innovations associated with (though not unique to) the Syriac scripts: the use of diacritics and the use of vowel-signs. Diacritics are distinguishing marks added to letters or words to differentiate forms which could be confused. The simplest example is the case of letters which, through a long process of development involving strong cursive tendencies, become indistinguishable. The problem is well known to teachers trying to read their pupils' handwriting! In several of the late Aramaic scripts, the letters **d** and **r** had become indistinguishable. Even in Nabataean and in Palmyrene sporadic attempts were made to use diacritics to solve the problem. In Syriac, a simple solution was universally used from a very early period: **d** had a dot added below it, **r** had a dot added above it.

In the Syriac script this is the only pair of letters which presented a serious problem. Other potential confusions are resolved by the fact that the method of joining letters together is very strict. Thus **q** and **w** are very similar, but the rules about joining and about final forms mean that it is always clear which is meant. But there are other types of potential confusion in Syriac. In a text without any vowels marked, it is usually impossible to distinguish, except by context, a singular from a plural noun, since the difference lies in the vocalisation (the vowels). Thus Syriac developed a double-dot mark, placed above nouns and occasionally verbal forms, to indicate a plural. Similarly, diacritic dots were used to distinguish the Syriac words for 'his' and 'her' and to distinguish the past tense of the verb from the participle, again because the differences lay in the vocalisation alone.

The real solution to problems of this kind had to lie in the invention of a system of marking vowels. The introduction of vowel-signs rendered most of the diacritics redundant, though not the diacritics for **d** and **r**, and diacritic dots were used to distinguish ordinary from aspirated pronunciation of /b/, /g/, /d/, /k/, /p/, /t/ (see Hebrew above).

Syriac ended up with two systems of vowel-notation. The one used in the East, which developed from as early as the fourth to fifth centuries AD, was an extension of the use of diacritic dots and consisted of patterns of dots (single and double) above and below consonants to indicate the vowel following the consonant. The consonants **w**, **y**, and **'** had already come to be used to indicate /ū/ō/, /ī/ē/ and /ā/ē/. This covered a wide range of distinctions between vowels, and it was this system which seems to have inspired the Hebrew vocalisation systems (see above).

In the West there emerged a system – traditionally attributed to Jacob of Edessa (d. AD 708), fragments of whose grammatical works survive, and definitely in use from *c.* AD 700 – in which the Greek letters **A**, **E** (in the form ε), **H** (/ē/, in later Greek /ī/), **O** and the combination **OU** (Greek OY, pronounced /oo/) were used to represent the vowels /a/, /e/, /i/, /o/ (pronounced like the vowel in 'raw') and /u/. They were written in very small script above or below the consonant after which the vowel was to be pronounced. While not perfect in that it does not make all necessary distinctions (so that certain of the older dot-signs remained in use), it *is* as good as the system used for English, in which it is equally true that not all necessary distinctions are seen in spelling (compare the different pronunciations of the letter **e** in 'the cat', 'the apple', 'then, 'they').

Syriac has the distinction of being the probable originator of vowel-notation by supralinear and sublinear markings. Both Hebrew and Arabic owe to Syriac their inspiration in this regard.

Syriac-speaking communities have survived in large numbers in the area around the point where the borders of Syria, Turkey and Iraq meet, and there are also *emigré* communities in Europe and the United States. Books, magazines and newspapers are still produced in the Syriac scripts.

A small number of scholars have argued that the Arabic script, which is quite unrelated to the older South Arabian script (above), was derived from the Syriac. In fact, it seems that there are a number of influences at work in the development of the Arabic script. One of these may well be awareness by the Arabs in the great cultural centres such as Damascus of the strong Syriac tradition of calligraphy, i.e. decorative writing, especially in fine copies of literary works. Syriac influence is also likely in the development of the Arabic diacritics and the vowel-system – a mixture of direct influence and analogical formation. It seems, however, that the origins of the Arabic script do not lie in Syriac alone.

Although the Arabs are known to have been present as an identifiable group from as early as the Assyrian period (in the ninth to seventh centuries BC), they did not become prominent historically until about the time of Christ. In this later period there was a strong Arab presence in the Hellenised cities of the Middle East such as Edessa and Palmyra (see map p. 8), where both Greek and Aramaic scripts were in use.

The first independent and clearly defined northern Arab kingdom known to us is that of the Nabataeans, centred on Petra in modern Jordan. Although known by their local tribal names (Nabaṭu and Šalamu), the Nabataeans were certainly Arabs, and they spoke a form of the Arabic language. For their inscriptions, however, they used the Aramaic which had become established as a language of colonial administration under the Assyrians and Persians. The fact that the Nabataeans normally spoke Arabic is reflected in the intrusion of certain distinctively Arabic forms and words into the Aramaic of their inscriptions. When eventually the Arabs in the region began to experiment for the first time with writing Arabic, they used the Nabataean Aramaic script which was familiar to them.

The Nabataean Aramaic script, derived ultimately from the earlier Aramaic script in use under the Persian Empire, is best known (as we have seen) from the first century AD. It is found in two forms. The formal script was used for monumental inscriptions, quite common on tombs, especially at Petra and at Madā'in Ṣāliḥ in Saudi Arabia. Alongside this formal script is a cursive script used principally on papyrus, of which we have a few precious surviving examples. The cursive script is continuous and flowing, with a regular pattern of joining of letters. The difference between the cursive and formal scripts is analogous to the difference between normal handwriting and the careful 'book-hand' one might use for a public notice. The cursive style tended to influence the formal script more and more in the first four centuries AD, and the Nabataean script developed into a cursive forerunner of the Arabic script.

However, some of the forms closest to Arabic already appear in the texts of the first century AD, so it is likely that there was a continuous tradition of writing on papyrus or parchment leading to the writing of Arabic texts, though little has survived. During this period, the first half of the first millennium AD, the Arabic language was spreading into the area of Palestine, Jordan

35 Nabataean tomb inscription from Madeba, 1st century AD. Louvre AO 4454

36 Early monumental and cursive Nabataean.

Dates AD	4/5	72/3	90/100	125		146/7	
ʾ							
b							
g							
d							
h							
w							
z							
ḥ							
ṭ							
y							
k							
l							
m							
n							
s							
ʿ							
p							
ṣ							
q							
r				ן = br			
š							
t							

Dates AD	Monumental 1st century	Cursive 1st/2nd century	211/2	265/6	266/8	305/7	328/9	Arabic
ʾ								
h								
w								
ṭ								
y								
m								
ʿ								
p								
š								
t								

37 Typical Nabataean forms approximating to Arabic.

38 The Namāra inscription (Arabic language, Nabataean script), AD 328–9.

and Syria, replacing the older (Arabian) languages of the area as well as Aramaic, which had become traditional. The early surviving Arabic texts were carved on stone. The very earliest to use the Nabataean Aramaic script – setting aside a short and disputed first-century AD inscription – comes from the mid-third century AD (AD 267–8), though the most famous example, the text from Namāra in southern Syria, is dated to AD 328–9. The latest dated Nabataean text comes from AD 355–6.

It seems that the Nabataean script lies at the origin of the Arabic script, but there are still some unresolved problems about the early development of the latter. Firstly, there is the chronological gap between the fourth century AD (the Namāra inscription and the last-dated Nabataean inscription) and the seventh, when papyri and inscriptions in Arabic proper become common. This can be partly bridged by the evidence of further transitional scripts in a group of short Arabic inscriptions from Zebed (AD 512), Ḥarrān, south of Damascus (AD 568) and Umm al-Jimāl (earlier a quite important Nabataean centre). Though rather scattered, these help to provide a link.

Secondly, there seem to have been from the beginning of the Islamic period several forms of the Arabic script. The so-called 'western cursive' script is the one most closely connected with Nabataean. The similarities are also ref-

39 Qur'ān in Naskhī script, 14th century AD.
BL Or 12809 f214a

lected in the more developed *naskhī* (Meccan-Medinan) script used in many
fine manuscripts. This form of Arabic script must represent the outcome of
a continuous tradition of writing in Nabataeo-Arabic in the Ḥijāz-Jordan-Syria
area. In the East a slightly different script came to be called Kūfic (named
after, though not directly linked with, Kūfa in Iraq); this may have arisen
from an offshoot of the Nabataean script and may have been more strongly
influenced by Syriac models.

We have noted earlier the development of diacritics in Syriac. There were
also early attempts at diacritics in Palmyrene, Nabataean and other late Aramaic
scripts. Thus the latest dated Nabataean inscription has a diacritic to distinguish
d and **r**. It was especially in the cursive ligatured scripts that problems of
differentiating between letters arose. In Nabataean, the following pairs came
to be hard to distinguish: **b/n, g/ḥ, z/r, y/t, p/q.**

39

40

40 Qur'ān in Kūfic
script, 9th century AD.
BL Or 1397 f18b

As the earlier script began to be used for Arabic, another problem was added to this. Arabic has a richer variety of consonantal sounds and needed twenty-eight consonants instead of the existing twenty-two. Hence, probably inspired by Nabataean and/or Syriac, Arabic used diacritic dots, firstly to distinguish certain letters (for example, z and r – z with a dot above, r without dot), and secondly to create new consonants; for example, a dot was added above the basic shape of ʻayn, ʻ, in order to create a further letter ġayn, ġ, since the sound /ġ/ did not exist in Aramaic and had no letter to represent it. A new ordering of the consonantal alphabet was also established, largely on the basis of the shapes of the letters (right to left):

اب ت ث ج ح خ د ذ ر ز س ش ص ض ط ظ ع غ ف ف ق ك ل م ن ه و ي

y w h n m l k q f ġ ʻ ẓ ṭ ḍ ṣ š s z r ḏ d ḫ ḥ j ṯ t b ʼ

It may be noted that the exact forms differ according to whether the letter is in initial, final or medial position in a word.

Finally, like Syriac, Arabic developed a system of marking vowels by the use of supralinear and sublinear marks. The three basic signs used, ˊ , ˌ and ٯ , are probably derived from letters of the Arabic alphabet. This is obvious for ٯ , from the Arabic w (و), though the other two forms are stylised. The three signs stand for short /a/, /i/ and /u/. The sign for /i/ is sublinear and the other two are supralinear. They could be lengthened if combined with the 'vowel-letters' ʼ, y and w to produce /ā/, /ī/ and /ū/. In addition, special signs were devised to indicate the doubling of a consonant (represented only by dots in Hebrew and Syriac) and to indicate the absence of any vowel after a consonant (ambiguously represented in Hebrew, and not in Syriac at all).

The Arabic script was, of course, widely used among the non-Arab peoples who accepted Islam. The most important offshoots of the script are the Persian and Ottoman Turkish varieties. Extra diacritics were devised to represent sounds which Arabic did not need to represent (i.e. for Persian /p/, /ch/, /j/ [as in French *jour*], /g/; for Turkish the same four plus /ng[n]/).

Arabic, Persian and Turkish manuscripts are notable for their use of calligraphy ('beautiful writing'), though the calligraphic tradition extends back to the Greco-Roman period. Sometimes there is evidence of calligraphy even in inscriptions on stone. The Nabataean tomb-inscriptions provide a good example. The earliest and best-attested calligraphic manuscripts in the Semitic languages are the ones in Syriac. Islam, however, took up the calligraphic tradition and made it its own in a special way. In some Muslim circles there was a reluctance to paint pictures of religious themes. As a result the artistic spirit of the Arabs was poured into abstract decoration and calligraphy.

29,35
33

Examples of Letters

Having surveyed the developments leading to the formation of the Greek and Latin alphabets on the one hand and the Hebrew and Arabic alphabets on the other, we have in the process also touched on the roles played by a number of 'minor' alphabets. In the light of this general survey it may be useful to look in some detail at a few of the individual letters of our own alphabet, tracing their origin back to the beginnings of alphabetic writing. There is only space here for a few examples and these have been chosen primarily for the relative simplicity of their history. Some letters are much more complex, and some letters of our alphabet have a relatively short history (i.e. **J** and **W**).

B

The pictograph derived from Egyptian was the picture of a house: ⌐⌐. In the transmission of the sign to the Proto-Sinaitic/Proto-Canaanite alphabet, the sign stood for **b**, the first letter of the West Semitic word for 'house', *bēt*. The box-like shape is best preserved in the South Arabian script, in which **b** is Π , and this is reflected in the Ethiopic **ቤ** , the Ethiopic script having been derived directly from the South Arabian. In the system of vowel-markings devised for Ethiopic, the different forms of this letter are **በ ቡ ቢ ባ ቤ ብ ቦ** . In Ugaritic, **b** is 𒌋𒌋 and this may be a cuneiform version, turned upside down, of the Π Π found in South Arabian and Ethiopic. It is also quite similar to the original pictograph.

In later Proto-Canaanite and in Phoenician, the letter changed to ◣ then ◿ , and stabilised as ƪ , the form which is standard in Phoenician, Hebrew, Moabite etc. This is the form taken over by Greek, though with a number of variations such as ⌐ and 𐌁 . Eventually it settled, with the fixing of the direction of writing, to become **B**, which has persisted into Latin and the European alphabets.

Within the West Semitic tradition the letter continued to evolve and in the Aramaic script it began to change quite dramatically. As in the case of a number of other letters, Aramaic began to open the closed loop at the top of the letter. This tendency may be related to the speed of writing in a highly cursivised form and to the materials used, especially papyrus. Whatever the cause, the opening of the top of the letter produced ﾞ , then ﾞ , then ﾞ , then ﾞ . The **b** in the Jewish (Hebrew) script was eventually formalised as ב , while in the other Aramaic scripts a variety of forms emerged. In Syriac (in all three types of script) we find ܒ and in formal Nabataean ב and in the cursive ﺏ (final ﺏ). The classic form of the letter in the cursive Arabic script is ﺏ , the dot being added to distinguish it from other letters. The dot was essential when the letter was joined to others: e.g. ﺒ = **b**: ﻨ = **n**!

57

N

N is derived from a pictograph of a snake (*nahaš*), basically a wiggly line: ٦ . This is still reflected in Ugaritic ▷▷— and as the scripts developed this became in Phoenician ٦ , in Hebrew ٦ and in Aramaic] . The same basic shape is retained by South Arabian ५ and Ethiopic ٦ ٦ ٤ ٩ ٤ ٦ ٩ .

In Greek we have the forms ᴎ and ᴎ , eventually levelled or balanced as **N**.

In the Aramaic tradition there are completely different developments: ٦ became] (Jewish: J) and then ⌐ (final]). In Syriac and Nabataean it became a single short vertical stroke (⌐ / ⌐), which, when joined (⌐⌐) was identical with several other letters including **B**. In Arabic it was distinguished by the addition of a single diacritic above it: ⌐ .

R

R is more complex. It originally depicted a human head (*rā'š/rō'š*) – in pictographic form ஃ . This was stylised as ٩ . Thus in Phoenician and Hebrew we find ٩ , with gradual opening of the head in Phoenician to produce ٦ (Ugaritic ᴃᴃ— ; South Arabian ১).

The letter entered the Greek alphabet as **P**, with a minor variant ʀ . Latin adopted and developed the variant form.

Aramaic opened the loop at the top, producing ५ , then ٦ , then ٦ (Jewish ٦). **R** and **D** ended up virtually identical, for example in Nabataean (٦) and Syriac (⊤ , *serṭā* ১). Diacritics were added, at first irregularly, but then in Syriac systematically to distinguish r (⊣ / ⊣) from d (⊤ / ?). In cursive Nabataean ٦ became ⌐ , then ⌐ , which is the Arabic form (⌐ when joined). In Arabic it had to be differentiated from z: a dot was added to z (⌐).

O

O is an even more complicated case, since its origin is a West Semitic *consonant* called (in Hebrew) *'ayin*. The name *'ayin* means 'eye' and the first letter of the Semitic word, transliterated as ', was pronounced as a constricted, almost strangulated, version of the glottal stop (/'/, see above). The original pictograph is, as might be expected, the picture of an eye: ⊂⊃ , gradually rounded to ⊙ and eventually losing its dot (as the pictographic aspect was forgotten). The Ugaritic ◁ is a cuneiform attempt to reproduce the circle and the circular shape is retained in South Arabian (○) and in Ethiopic, where the forms with vowels are *ዐ ዐ ዒ ዓ ዔ ዕ ዖ* . The Ethiopic series illustrates well how the addition of the vowel-marker in that script could lead to fairly complicated variations in the basic letter.

In Greek, too, the circle is retained. Some archaic scripts have the dot in the middle, reflecting a very early form of the letter (though note that the dotted form was still in use in the eastern Aramaic script as late as the ninth century BC). But Greek had no /ʻ/-sound and used O as a vowel, as we still do in the Latin alphabet. At a second stage Greek modified the O to produce Ω, representing long /ō/.

Meanwhile, in the Semitic area, O continued to be used for /ʻ/. It is again in Aramaic that the changes occurred. As in other cases, Aramaic opened the closed loop at the top producing ○ . When this was written in two strokes it became ∪ , then y , then y (the form in the Jewish script). In later Aramaic dialects two forms were prevalent, the Syriac ⊾ and the Nabataean ✓ , which became ✓ , then ✓ , then Arabic ع .

H

In the case of H, as in several other cases in the transmission of the alphabet between languages (notably in the case of the various Semitic /s/-sounds), there has been some switching of usage. The sign from which H developed is ▥ , probably originally depicting a fence. In the Phoenician tradition the form changed to ⊟ , then ⊟ . The sound it represented – transcribed as /ḥ/ – is a roughly breathed aitch.

Some archaic Greek scripts used for dialects which preserved an /h/-sound used the sign as H for the so-called rough breathing, a breathy aitch found at the beginning of many Greek words. But it was not used for this in Ionic Greek (which lacked this sound) or in the later Greek script (in which a reversed apostrophe, ʻ, came to be used for the rough breathing). Instead, H was used to represent the long vowel /ē/ (later /ī/). In Latin it again reverted to use as a consonant.

In the Aramaic tradition the letter became ⊓ (Jewish script ⊓) and in later Aramaic we find Syriac ᴗ (through reduction of size and joining up) and Nabataean ⋈ , which became ⋀ and in cursive forms ⋋ and ⋋ . The Arabic is close to this with ⊃ (final ⊂), but at first this sign had to do duty for both /ḥ/ and for /ḫ/, a consonantal sound which Arabic has but none of the Aramaic scripts represent. Its sound is more rasping than /ḥ/, more like the /ch/ in the Scottish 'loch'. In due course Arabic devised a diacritic above the letter to indicate /ḫ/, leaving /ḥ/ unmarked. (In a separate development, g also ended up with the same basic shape and was given a sublinear diacritic).

It may be noted that both /ḥ/ and /ḫ/ did exist in Ugaritic, South Arabian and Ethiopic, though the relation of the forms to the tradition described above is hard to explain. Thus /ḥ/ is ⊳╪⊲ in Ugaritic, ¥ in South Arabian and ḥ in Ethiopic, while for /ḫ/ we have ⚡ , ⋎ and ⋏ .

Excursus: Use of the Alphabet for Numerals

The older, syllabic writing systems of the ancient Near East had their own methods of using various signs to indicate numerals without having to write the words out in full. In the common West Semitic tradition, a single vertical stroke represented **1** and other strokes were added to produce the numbers up to **9**. **10** has a sign of its own (usually ⌐ originally a horizontal line) and so does **20** (⌐ʒ originally two horizontal lines). The larger numbers are simply formed by placing the numbers side by side: **14** = ⫠⫠ ⌐.

It appears that the Greeks used two systems. The older one, dating to the seventh century BC, is acrophonic – i.e. the first letter of the word used for the numeral was used as a sign for that numeral. Thus 'ten' is in Greek *deka* (Δέχα) and the sign for **10** is *Δ*. For 'one' a simple vertical stroke was used. The other system, traditionally connected with Miletus and in use at least from the second century BC, gives numerical values to each of the letters of the alphabet; **a** to **th** (α – θ, including the archaic *digamma*) are used for **1 – 9**, **i – r** (ι – ρ, including the archaic q) for **10, 20, 30**, etc. to **100** and **s** to archaic *san* (σ –⅄) for **200, 300**, etc. to **900**. Use of *digamma*, the old **q** and *san* (of Phoenician origin) suggest an origin where these three survived in use.

The Roman numerals are still in use and current usage needs no introduction. It should, however, be noted that the origins of **M, D, C, L**, etc. are very complex. For example, **D (500)** is actually not a letter but half of an old sign for **1000**, ⊂⊃ . These signs gradually became assimilated to letters of the alphabet though they are not alphabetic in origin.

It was from Greek influence in the Hellenistic period that the alphabetic numeral system was adopted by Hebrew and Aramaic. In Hebrew, ' – ṭ = **1 – 9**, **y – ṣ** = **10, 20, ...90**, and **q – t** = **100, 200, 300, 400** (**tq = 500** and so on). Thus **y' = 11** and **qy' = 111**. Diacritic dots were put over the unit letters to turn them into thousands: אַ̈ = **1000**. Similarly Syriac, also under Greek influence, began to use the equivalent letters, abandoning the older system (see above). In Arabic, prior to the import from India of the system we call the Arabic numerals (since we got them from the Arabs), the same alphabetic system was used, exactly as in Hebrew and Syriac. Arabic even adopted the alphabetic order of these other scripts for this purpose, despite the fact that this did not correspond to the new Arabic alphabetic order based on letter-shape. The Ethiopic script also used the same system, but retained the Greek letters for this purpose, so clearly the alphabetic character of the numerals had ceased to be significant.

Relationship between Main Scripts

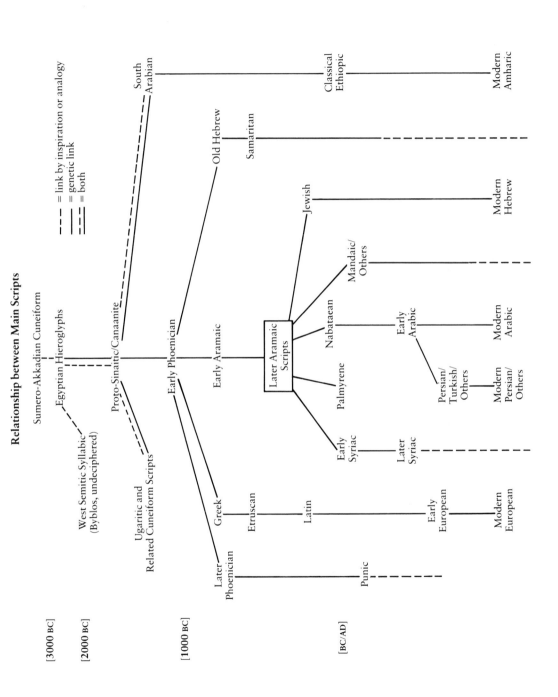

[3000 BC]

[2000 BC]

[1000 BC]

[BC/AD]

- - - - = link by inspiration or analogy

———— = genetic link

══════ = both

Sumero-Akkadian Cuneiform

Egyptian Hieroglyphs

West Semitic Syllabic (Byblos, undeciphered)

Ugaritic and Related Cuneiform Scripts

Proto-Sinaitic/Canaanite

South Arabian

Classical Ethiopic

Modern Amharic

Old Hebrew

Samaritan

Early Phoenician

Early Aramaic

Jewish

Modern Hebrew

Later Aramaic Scripts

Mandaic/ Others

Nabataean

Early Arabic

Modern Arabic

Palmyrene

Persian/ Turkish/ Others

Modern Persian/ Others

Early Syriac

Later Syriac

Greek

Etruscan

Latin

Early European

Modern European

Later Phoenician

Punic

Summary and Conclusions

In the short space available here we have covered a wide range of topics, concentrating on the earliest attempts at alphabetic writing, the development of the West Semitic scripts and the transmission of the alphabet to the Greeks, the later Semitic scripts and the origins of the Arabic script. A number of general points have been made in the process.

The two great pivotal moments in this story are the devising of the consonantal alphabet on an acrophonic basis in the early second millennium BC, and the addition of the vowels to the consonantal repertoire in the earlier part of the first millennium BC. The first of these steps forward we owe to some uncertain group of inventors, possibly in a scribal school in Palestine, Phoenicia or Syria. The second we owe to the Greeks. The only other invention in this field which is more important than either of these is the invention of writing itself, probably in Mesopotamia in the late fourth millennium BC.

From these developments have come enormous benefits for mankind. We are ourselves still using a developed form of the same alphabet tradition. But it is not only the long-standing character of this invention which should be noted, nor its wide distribution and its adaptability to languages which have only recently been written down. After all, cuneiform was widespread, lasted three thousand years and was used for such diverse languages as Sumerian, Akkadian and Hittite. Rather, the great contribution of the development of the alphabet was the fact that its simplicity was the first and necessary prerequisite of universal literacy.

Once the alphabet was available, virtually anyone could learn to read and write. It was no longer necessary to undergo a lengthy training, and literacy could therefore no longer easily be controlled by a scribal élite. In ancient times, holy books and books of philosophy were at last open to all. In more recent times, before the advent of sound media such as radio and television, ideas disseminated through books, pamphlets, posters and newspapers led to major political changes including the American War of Independence and the French and Russian Revolutions. Indeed, the immense possibilities inherent in each individual's being able to read and write – to transmit and receive information at will – have yet to be exhausted even now, four thousand years later.

Further Reading

P. C. Craigie, *Ugarit and the Old Testament* (Grand Rapids, 1983)

M. Dietrich and O. Loretz, *Die Keilalphabete: die phönizisch-kanaanäischen und altarabischen Alphabete in Ugarit* (Münster, 1988)

D. Diringer, *The Alphabet: A Key to the History of Mankind*, (London, 3rd edn 1968)

D. Diringer, *Writing* (London, 1962)

G. R. Driver, *Semitic Writing from Pictograph to Alphabet* (London, 3rd edn 1976)

A. Gaur, *A History of Writing* (London, 1984)

I. J. Gelb, *A Study of Writing* (Chicago/London, 2nd edn 1963)

S. A. Kaufmann, 'The Pitfalls of Typology: On the Early History of the Alphabet', *Hebrew Union College Annual* 57 (1986), pp. 1–14

A. G. Loundine, 'L'abécédaire de Beth Shemesh', *Le Muséon* 100 (1987), pp. 243–50

A. R. Millard, 'The Canaanite Linear Alphabet and its Passage to the Greeks', *Kadmos* 15 (1976), pp. 130–44

J. Naveh, *The Development of the Aramaic Script* (Jerusalem, 1970)

J. Naveh, *Early History of the Alphabet: An Introduction to West Semitic Epigraphy and Palaeography* (Jerusalem/Leiden, 1982)

J. Naveh, 'Proto-Canaanite, Archaic Greek, and the Script of the Aramaic Text on the Tell Fakhariyah Statue' in *Ancient Israelite Religion: Essays in Honor of Frank Moore Cross*, ed. P. D. Miller *et al.* (Philadephia, 1987), pp. 101–13

E. Puech, 'Origine de l'alphabet', *Revue Biblique* 93 (1986), pp. 161–213

J. Ryckmans, 'L'ordre alphabétique sud-sémitique et ses origines', in *Mélanges linguistiques offerts à Maxime Rodinson* (Paris, 1985), pp. 343–59.

J. Ryckmans, 'A. G. Lundin's Interpretation of the Beth Shemesh Abecedary: A Presentation and Commentary', *Proceedings of the Seminar for Arabian Studies* 18 (1988), pp. 123–29

Y. H. Safadi, *Islamic Calligraphy* (London, 1978)

B. Sass, *The Genesis of the Alphabet and its Development in the Second Millennium BC* (Wiesbaden, 1988)

Note also in this series, *Reading the Past*:

L. Bonfante, *Etruscan* (London, 1990)

B. F. Cook, *Greek Inscriptions* (London, 1987)

W. V. Davies, *Egyptian Hieroglyphs* (London, 1987)

O. A. W. Dilke, *Mathematics and Measurement* (London, 1987)

R. I. Page, *Runes* (London, 1987)

J. Reynolds, *Latin Inscriptions* (London, forthcoming 1991)

C. B. F. Walker, *Cuneiform* (London, 1987)

Index